The Chamonix Valley

A Mad Dog Ski guide

Published by Mad Dog Ski
maddogski.com

Mad Dog Ski
The Chamonix Valley
First edition 2009

Published by Mad Dog Ski
Town maps © Mad Dog Ski
Piste map © Atelier Esope

Writers: Laura Rees and Tom Wilson-North
Editors: Kate Whittaker and Tory Dean
Design: David Marshall
Artwork: Ian Stratford
Printed by: CPG, Tonbridge

ISBN 978-0-9558065-0-6

A catalogue record of this book is available at the British Library.

Mad Dog Ski, P O Box 236, Heald Green, Cheadle, SK8 3YQ, UK
maddogski.com
+44 (0)845 054 2906

All rights reserved. No part of this publication may be reproduced or transmitted in any form or by any means, electronically or mechanically, including photography, recording or any information storage or retrieval system without prior written permission from the publisher. No part of this publication may be used in any form of advertising sales promotion or publicity without prior written permission from the publisher.

Contents

Don't miss our handy quick reference sections...

Resort map 22

Where to ski? 30

Avalanche! 38

Lift pass prices 46

Our favourite restaurants 75

Resort restaurants map 72

Our favourite bars 83

Après-ski map 84

About Mad Dog Ski

About our books 8

Snow & weather reports 9

Our Chamonix researchers 10

About Chamonix

The resort 13

Getting there 14

Resort maps 18/22

The villages 19

Where to stay 21

On the piste

The ski area 29

Getting on the slopes 33

Beginners 35

Intermediate 36

Advanced 36

Off-piste 37

Safety 38

Mountain guides 43

Snowboarders 44

Cross-country 45

Lift passes 46

Weather 47

Ski and snowboard school 48

maddogski.com

On the piste (continued)

Equipment hire 49

Piste rankings 51

Day trips 58

Food and drink

Vegetarian options 67

Budget meals and take-aways ... 67

Local specialities 68

Resort restaurants 74

Après-ski and nightlife 82

Mountain restaurants 89

Other things to do

Non-skiing activities 97

Shopping 101

Children

Accommodation 107

Child-friendly tour operators 111

Childcare 112

Ski school 112

Activities 112

Restaurants 112

The list

Our essential resort directory ... 113

Maps

Chamonix Town 22

Chamonix Valley 18

Resort restaurants 72

Resort bars and clubs 84

Mountain restaurants 90

About Mad Dog Ski guidebooks and how they'll make a real difference to your holidays.

What you'll find in this chapter

About this book 8
Snow and weather reports 9
About our researchers 10

About Mad Dog Ski

My time in the mountains used to be restricted to one or two precious weeks a year. Each winter, I would arrive eager to get on the slopes as soon as possible, indulge in some good après-ski and ensure we had somewhere decent to refuel at lunchtime. All too often, this precious information comes the day before you have to head home.

During my first season as a 30-something chalet host, I realised I wasn't alone in my quest for reliable information. Week after week guests would ask the same questions; where should they ski, where were the best places to eat and drink, the best mountain restaurants? Mad Dog Ski was born.

Now that we've published guidebooks to nine ski resorts, plus one on our favourite ski weekends, we feel ready to take on the challenge of pinning Chamonix down in print. Unique amongst resorts, the buzz that comes from the combination of a larger town and amazing off-piste makes it somewhere that skiers and boarders from all over the world are drawn to. And many of them choose to stay. Our researchers Tom and Laura have lived in the resort for years so are perfectly placed to pass on inside information on both the town and the mountains.

With Mad Dog Ski, we always give you our independent view. Extra special places that our researchers return to again and again are marked throughout the book as 'Mad Dog favourites'. If our taste differs from yours or if you find places we haven't, please email us at **info@maddogski.com**. Enjoy the mountain!

Kate Whittaker
Founder, Mad Dog Ski

maddogski.com

About this book

Mad Dog books are designed to be of most use when you get to Chamonix. Packed with the essentials for when you're in resort, they're still small enough for your ski jacket pocket. For the full lowdown on planning your trip (your travel options, where to stay etc) check out **maddogski.com**. If you can't find what you're looking for, or have a tricky question, email us from our homepage.

Prices

Prices are based on the 2008/9 season. Prices for food, drink and services in resort are given in euro (€). At the time of going to print the sterling exchange rate was £1 = €1.09.

Skier or snowboarder?

Whether you board or ski, throughout the book we use 'skiing' and 'skier' as interchangeable terms for 'riding' and 'boarder'. No offence is intended – it just seems easier.

Children

Whilst Chamonix isn't exactly a family resort, there are always plenty of kids around and so the majority of places are very welcoming. Our kids symbol (☺) shows restaurants and services which we think are child-friendly.

For more tips and ideas on family skiing holidays, including checklists, what to do and where to eat see the **Children** chapter and **maddogski.com**.

Telephone numbers

French numbers in this book are prefixed by the international dialling code +33 (ie 00 33). To call France from the UK dial +33 and drop the first zero of the French number. From France to the UK, dial +44 and drop the first zero of the UK area code.

You'll find public telephones that accept phone cards throughout the resort. Buy your phone card from a tabac. It may be helpful to know that French mobile numbers always start with '06'.

Snow and weather reports

See **maddogski.com** for snow reports and webcams. You can also keep up to date at **chamonix-meteo.com**.

We're not perfect

Finally, whilst we make every effort to get things right, prices and opening times can change from season to season. If you spot an error or have a different opinion to us, please let us know using **info@maddogski.com**.

About Mad Dog Ski

About our researchers

Laura Rees

Laura is embarking on her fifth season in Chamonix after swapping a career in marketing in central London for a career in marketing in Chamonix. She's proud of her Welsh roots and lives and breathes the mountain lifestyle as much as she can. Laura's a former equestrian pro who's just as much at home in a pair of snowboard bindings as a saddle and stirrups.

Best restaurant Satsuki for quality Japanese food
Best après-ski Chambre Neuf; the original and still the best
Favourite lunch stop Les Houches' hidden gem Les Vielles Luges
Best run Belle Place at Le Tour - wide, undulating, challenging but not too terrifying

Tom Wilson-North

Brit Tom joined the team in 2006 but has been living in the mountains for many years following a career as a concierge in London. He's lived in Chamonix since 2006, as according to him it's the 'best place in the world'. He's a qualified snowboard instructor, an avid downhill mountain biker and a secret fan of Dire Straits.

Best restaurant Munchie, for the Korean hot pot
Best après-ski MBC. Great beer, awesome bar snacks, not too many people
Favourite lunch stop L'Arret Bougnete at Vallorcine station, between the railway track and the gondola
Best run Anywhere on the back side of Les Grands Montets down to the glacier

Mad Dog Ski Chamonix

Chamonix; the inside view of what makes this resort different.

What you'll find in this chapter

The resort 13
Getting there 14
Resort maps 18/22
The villages 19
Where to stay 21

About Chamonix

Ask anyone who's been to Chamonix what it's like, and you'll get chapter and verse on its many charms. The deep valley in the shadow of Western Europe's highest mountain is a land of glaciers, frozen waterfalls, seracs and crevasses, and of simple access to the highest peaks.

Chamonix is a long, natural valley with villages dotted up and down its length. Visitors stay in Chamonix town or one of the major outlying villages like Argentière, Les Houches or Le Tour. The valley is nestled into a corner of France, with Switzerland just to one side and Italy a short distance to the other.

Back in 1924, Chamonix was home to the first ever Winter Olympics, which placed the town at the very centre of mountain activity. And it's been the same ever since. It's a unique combination of year-round tourist destination and purpose-built winter resort. At a shade over 1000m, much lower than many Alpine resorts, the valley floor usually escapes the heavy snowfall of higher altitudes, making travelling about much easier. So much the better, because the different ski areas are very spread out so every visitor will need to spend time getting around the valley. The bus service is normally first choice, though it comes under heavy criticism for being infrequent and unpunctual. Luckily, the train runs to time and stops near all of the valley's lift base stations.

Chamonix at a glance

- 155km of pistes
- 49 lifts
- Highest lift 3840m
- Vertical drop:
  2052m (Grands Montets)
  1490m (Brévent)
  1336m (Flégère)
  808m (Le Tour)
  2807m (Aguille du Midi)
  853m (Les Houches)
- Average annual snowfall 9.6m
- Population 9830

maddogski.com

Transport on both is free with the 'carte d'hôte' pass (available from your accommodation provider).

You may have noticed that Chamonix's official piste count is lower than other resorts. The natural, unpisted freeride terrain is really why people come here and it's what gives Chamonix its 'experts only' reputation. Don't be misled by the low number of true pistes; there is more than enough to keep a piste-cruiser entertained for a week.

Getting there

Geneva-Cointrin Airport (gva.ch) is in Switzerland, but only an hour's drive from Chamonix. The airport is serviced by regular airlines as well as the budget carriers.

Chamonix is the French side of the Mont Blanc Tunnel, one of the main transport arteries from France into Italy. There are plenty of Chamonix signs along all of the roads, and from Geneva it's motorway the whole way, which makes transfers or driving to the resort a breeze. In snowstorms, the road is usually top of the Haute Savoie priority list for ploughing meaning Chamonix almost never gets cut off.

Since the valley and the ski areas are spread out, lots of people opt to hire a car, especially if there are more than three in a group; it makes life much easier, it's not too expensive and parking is never too

Don't leave Chamonix without...

- doing a guided day on the Vallée Blanche from the Aiguille du Midi (p.42)
- visiting the Montenvers ice cave (p.101)
- eating at **Munchie** (p.79)
- taking in the glacier views of the **Point de Vue** piste (p.36)
- snow shoeing to **Les Vielles Luges** for dinner (p.94)
- experiencing après-ski at **Chambre Neuf** (p.85)

Mad Dog Ski Chamonix

Ski holidays have reached new heights

zenith holidays

Zenith Holidays present fantastic and unexpected resorts alongside the favourites you know and love. They make our grade because they have exceptional snow and more besides to make your holiday unforgettable.

Whether you are looking for a short break with friends or a week away with the family – start building your holiday at www.zenithholidays.co.uk/chamonix Creating your perfect holiday with our flexible system means that you get the best value for money allowing you to ***do more*** this season!

www.zenithholidays.co.uk   Tel: 01737 852242

ABTA Y1542

O T Chamonix Mt Blanc M Colonel

Airlines serving Geneva

Regular Airlines
Blue Islands (Channel Islands) blueislands.com
British Airways ba.com
Swiss swiss.com

Budget Carriers
Aer Lingus aerlingus.com
BMI Baby bmibaby.com
EasyJet easyjet.com
Flybe flybe.com
Globespan flyglobespan.com
Jet2.com jet2.com

much of a headache. If you do rent, make sure you pick your car up from the Swiss side of the airport, so it'll come with a 'vignette' sticker, which lets you use the Swiss motorways for free. Swiss rented cars also usually have snow tyres which are by no means standard on the French side (this is probably why the rental prices tend to be cheaper this side). If you do hire on the French side, you can buy a vignette at the border. Naturally, check for snow tyres and snow chains. And remember to tell the agency that you'll be staying over the border in France to make sure you get the right insurance.

Private transfers are by far the most popular way to get to Chamonix for those not wanting the hassle of a car. For collection from the airport you'll need to make a reservation in advance. Expect to pay between €25 and €40 per person for a transfer.

Transfer companies
Alpybus alpybus.com
A-T-S a-t-s.net
Cham Express chamexpress.com
Cham Shuttle chamonixshuttles.com
Chamvan cham-van.com
Mountain Drop-offs mountaindropoffs.com

About Chamonix

You can catch the public bus from Geneva to Chamonix for around €35 single (€55 return). The bus is operated by **SAT Mont Blanc** (sat-montblanc.com) and stops at the towns of Sallanches and Le Fayet on the way up, taking in all around two hours. There are three buses a day. Remember that whilst transfers will normally wait for you if you're delayed, the public bus definitely won't. Our advice; for the price difference involved, stick to the private transfers.

There is also a train option which, frankly, is not really an option as the most direct goes via Martigny and Vallorcine and takes close to four hours.

maddogski.com

Chamonix Valley

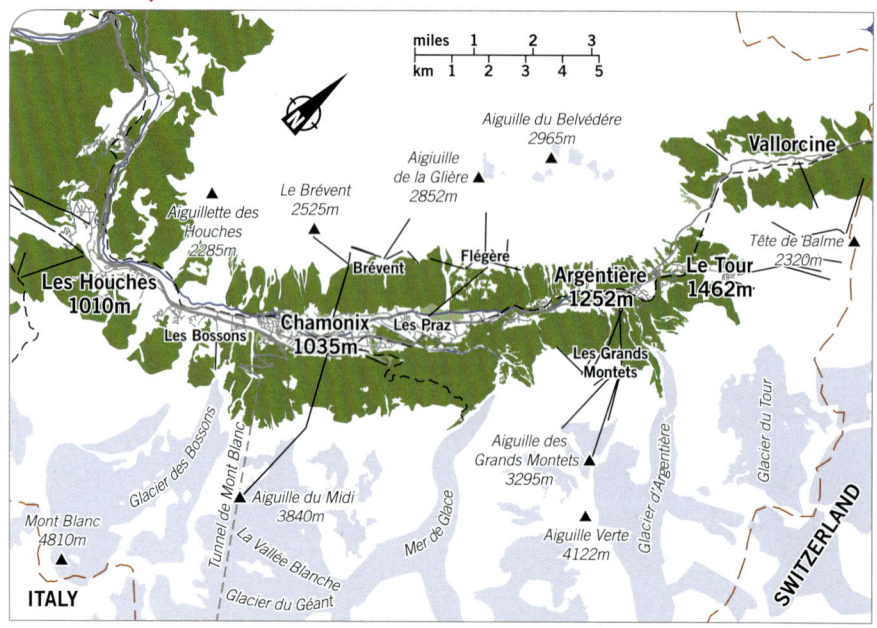

The villages

Chamonix

The sprawling centre of Chamonix is where most of the valley's accommodation is located. All the major services are here, as are the hotels, hostels and campsites. The Planpraz gondola, which whips skiers up to the Brévent area, is a 15 minute (uphill) walk or a short bus ride away. The Aiguille du Midi cable car, which serves both the Vallée Blanche (p.42) and Pré du Rocher freeride areas, is three minutes' walk from town. Morning sees skiers grabbing croissants and pack lunches at the bakeries (p.70), while at the other end of the day the town reverberates to the thud of live music from bars from about 4pm onwards as après-ski kicks off.

Chamonix Sud

Chamonix Sud is where you'll find the majority of low cost self-catering apartments. It's a stone's throw to the Aiguille du Midi cable car, and there are plenty of bars on the ground floor of the courtyards, so evenings are very busy with tourist and seasonnaire barhoppers.

Argentière

A 15 minute drive uphill from Chamonix, the valley's second biggest settlement is Argentière. With the peaks and glaciers of the Les Grands Montets ski area soaring up above the town and a lovely centre-valley situation ensuring maximum sunshine, it's little wonder that so many people choose to stay here. The vibe is more villagey, and lots of families prefer the calmer atmosphere of the place – it's also very convenient for the Les Grands Montets area, and not far from the sunny, child-friendly pistes of peaceful Le Tour.

The sloped main street is where you'll find the majority of restaurants, bars and hotels, though the old town – towards the highest part of the village – is perfect for an after-dinner wander. Since Argentière is over 200m higher than Chamonix, the snow falls deeper and hangs around longer. You're more likely to need snow boots and snow chains for getting around up here than down in the rest of the valley.

maddogski.com

Les Houches

As the most southerly and the lowest of the valley's villages, Les Houches is Chamonix's little sister. The spread-out village (a 20 minute bus ride from Chamonix) has accommodation and restaurants along the length of the main street, but the handful of bars are located in the St Antoine district. The Bellevue cable car and the Prarion gondola are about 500m apart, but they are linked by a bus service which runs a few times an hour.

Les Praz

Les Praz is a pretty hamlet of chalets, a couple of restaurants and a summertime golf course clustered around the bottom station of the Flégère cable car. A 10 minute riverside stroll from Chamonix town centre, Les Praz escapes the evening noise and bustle, whilst maintaining a central-ish location.

The Les Bois area of Les Praz is where many of the high end chalets and upmarket second homes can be found.

Le Tour

At the base of the Charamillon gondola at the top of the valley is the sleepy village of Le Tour. Even though it's about half a mile from the nearest station, it's well served by the resort bus and there's a couple of simple cafés serving snacks and ice creams around the gondola base. Heed the warnings about the increased snowfall in the Argentière section; the same applies up here at Le Tour, some 400m above Chamonix.

Vallorcine

Separated from Chamonix by the Col des Montets, Vallorcine (a derivative from the old French 'valley of the bears') is a beautiful mountain town at 1264m, the last bastion of French soil before you hit the Swiss border. The town has few restaurants, and next to no nightlife, so the 'action' is centred on the station and gondola base. From here, skiers can access the back side of Le Tour. Some 50m from the station, before the tourist office, is a great local bakery and lovely traditional butchers, who can knock you up a joint-effort, world-beating ham sandwich while you wait.

Where to stay

Accommodation in the Chamonix valley varies greatly in quality and convenience. Given the nature of the valley it can be difficult to find quality accommodation which is both close to the lifts and to the resort facilities. The main hotel and chalet operators, being very aware of this, tend to have the best locations with maximum convenience and minimum commuting. There is very little actual ski in, ski out accommodation, so you'll still have to do a certain amount of travelling to get on the mountain (p.33).

Hotels are a great option for those not wishing to book an entire property or join a mixed group. Have a look at Best Mont Blanc (**bestmontblanc.com**), which has four hotels across the resort including the Mont Blanc in the centre of town and the family-friendly Alpina (p.108).

Inghams (inghams.co.uk), **Crystal** (crystalski.co.uk), and **Esprit** (espritski.com) are the larger tour operators in the valley and, although an increasing number of people now arrange their own trips, they continue to offer ski packages at competitive prices. So far as families go, Esprit are very good with kids and the nannies are often seen guiding children on their adventures through the town while their parents are tearing up the slopes.

For those wanting a more flexible and personal touch, it's very simple to put together your own package. Try these places which have attained popularity through quirkiness, character and location. For more suggestions, including reviews and visitors' feedback, see **maddogski.com**.

Hotels

Chamonix

The Clubhouse
t +33 (0)4 50 90 96 56
w clubhouse.fr
74 Promenade des Sonnailles.
Chic, sophisticated, and linked to posh London members' club Milk & Honey, the Clubhouse is a lovely

Chamonix town centre – landmarks and hotels

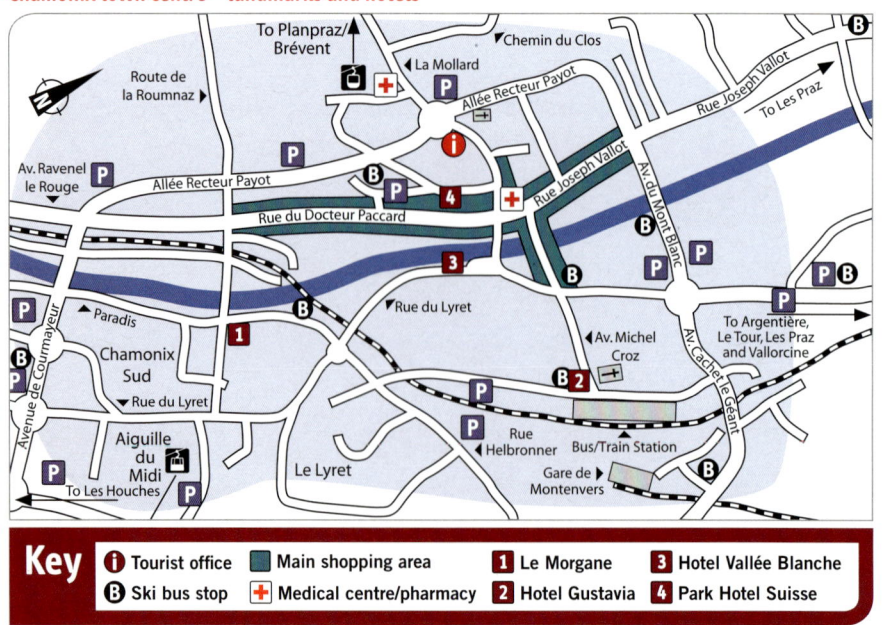

Key
- 🛈 Tourist office
- 🅱 Ski bus stop
- ✚ Medical centre/pharmacy
- **1** Le Morgane
- **2** Hotel Gustavia
- **3** Hotel Vallée Blanche
- **4** Park Hotel Suisse

hotel and the bar undoubtedly the place to be seen sipping a Margarita. Located near the eastern end of town, The Clubhouse is close to the nursery slopes and the ski bus stop.

Hotel Gustavia ***
t +33 (0)4 50 53 00 31
w hotel-gustavia.com

272 Avenue Michel Croz.
The best and worst thing about the Hotel Gustavia is that it is linked to the most popular bar in Chamonix, **Chambre Neuf**. True party animals will love knowing that bed is just a couple of seconds' scramble from the bar. Those wanting peace and quiet may prefer a hotel further from the hustle and bustle of a busy nightspot. Décor is stylish and the food great. Not recommended for families with young children because of the bar downstairs.

Le Morgane ****
t + 33 (0)4 50 53 57 15
w morgane-hotel-chamonix.com
145 Avenue de l'Aiguille du Midi.
Le Morgane is stylish and modern yet maintains a friendly ambience

Orientation: Chamonix's main landmarks and areas

- **Main square** Place Balmat next to the river, right in the centre of town
- **Main street** Rue du Docteur Paccard, which runs south-west from the main square
- **Post Office** in Place Balmat
- **Sports Centre** Centre Sportif Richard Bozon on Avenue de la Plage
- **Chamonix Sud** a high-rise complex of low-cost accommodation in the southern part of town, built around one major courtyard
- **Train station** La Gare SNCF, on Place de la Gare in the centre of town

maddogski.com

thanks to the warm, professional staff. Rooms are a good size and bathrooms are ensuite. There's a spa with pool, hammam and treatment rooms. The hotel's ground-floor restaurant is Le Bistrot, which has Michelin star winner Michaël Bourdillat at the helm.

Park Hotel Suisse ★★★
t +33 (0)4 50 53 07 58
w chamonix-park-hotel.com

Allée du Majestic.
Brilliantly situated in the centre of town, moments away from the nearest boulangerie and just a minute from the ski bus stop, the Park Suisse always seems to be full – no doubt because it is charming, with spacious bedrooms, a great restaurant and friendly staff.

Hotel Vallée Blanche ★★
t +33 (0)4 50 53 04 50
w vallee-blanche.com
36 Rue du Lyret.
No hotel is more central. Shops, restaurants and bars can be reached in seconds, while the bus stops are just a couple of minutes' walk away. The hotel has no dedicated restaurant though this matters little as there are several good restaurants nearby. Spot on for simple, comfortable and well located accommodation.

Argentière
Hotel Grands Montets ★★★
t +33 (0)4 50 54 06 66
w hotel-grands-montets.com

340 Chemin des Arbérons.
Ideally situated at the bottom of the Les Grands Montets cable car, the Hotel Grands Montets is a charming Alpine lodge just a few minutes' walk from the main street in Argentière.

Recommended for families because of the garden – just waiting for snowmen – and proximity to the Panda Club kids' ski school (p.112). The swimming pool and hot tub are also very popular.

About Chamonix

Luxury, style and comfort are the words that spring to mind when describing the tiny chalet village of Les Granges d'en Haut. Although built recently, the chalets remain true to the local surroundings and tradition. Each sleeps up to eight people and has its own personal sauna. There's also a spa, fabulous bar and restaurant. High-end, but highly recommended.

Les Houches

Hotel & Chalet du Bois ***
t +33 (0)4 50 54 50 35
w hotel-du-bois.com
475 Avenue des Alpages.
Located in the picturesque Les Houches, Hotel du Bois is nearer the bars and restaurants of the St Antoine district than the Prarion or Bellevue lifts (about 2km away). Fortunately the ski bus stops just outside, and the accommodation is as comfortable as the staff are friendly. Good for those wanting a more peaceful type of holiday.

Les Granges d'en Haut
t +33 (0)4 50 54 65 36
w grangesdenhaut.com
Route des Chavants (about 1km above the base of the Prarion lift).

Chalets

Chalet La Forêt
t +44 (0)754 557 5277
w chaletlaforet.com

Nestled amid forestry in the heart of the Chamonix valley is the charming Chalet la Forêt. Traditional (yet with a hot tub and sauna) and welcoming, the chalet

maddogski.com

is well situated for Les Praz and just a 10 minute walk from the Flégère ski lift and local bars and restaurants. Usually offered on a self-catered basis.

Demi Piste
t +33 (0)6 09 91 60 18
w demipiste.com
Debbie and Al run Chalet Blanche, a lovely eight bedroom catered chalet on the outskirts of town, and a number of other self-catered apartments dotted around the valley.

Hip Chalets
t + 33 (0)6 75 61 91 90
w hipchalets.com
The choice of celebrities in town, Hip Chalets has several luxury properties. Nothing is overlooked; each property is beautifully decorated, supremely comfortable and with fascinating history and individuality. No run-of-the-mill concrete block chalets here. Hip Chalets are expensive, high end places and usually run on a fully catered basis. If you have the cash, this is the place to splash it.

Ice & Orange
t +33 (0)4 50 90 87 17
w iceandorange.com
159 Route des Tissières, Les Bossons (towards Les Houches).
Ice & Orange own and run the Chalet Tissières, a large and impressive property that can sleep up to 24. The owners Damien and Renske are friendly and helpful, and the chalet well equipped and welcoming. A great choice for large groups or for those happy to share with others.

Mountain Retreats

t (0)1635 253946
w mountainretreats.co.uk
Mountain Retreats are a family-run chalet company with several chalets in Argentière and the surrounding area. The owners are friendly and helpful (especially for families with young children), chalets are stylish and the staff brilliantly trained.

This chapter is about getting you **on the piste** as quickly as possible; after all, that's why you're here.

What you'll find in this chapter

The ski area	29
Getting on the slopes	33
Beginners	35
Intermediates	36
Advanced	36
Off-piste	37
Safety	38
Mountain guides	43
Snowboarders	44
Cross-country	45
Lift passes	46
Weather	47
Ski and snowboard schools	48
Equipment hire	49
Piste rankings	51
Day trips	58

Despite its reputation as an experts-only destination, Chamonix still has plenty of blues and reds to keep intermediates busy… but it's the off-piste access and ski mountaineering that people really come for.

The ski area

Chamonix is a long, dramatic valley, running approximately 14km from north-east to south-west, and a mere 2km from side to side. The south-facing side is home to the non-glaciated areas of Brévent and La Flégère. At the north-east end of the valley is the mellow, horseshoe bowl of Le Tour, and at the far south-west is the small, lower area of Les Houches. Finally, on the north-facing side, you'll find the Grands Montets resort, which soars up above Argentière village, and the famous Aiguille du Midi cable car, which rises up from Chamonix town.

There are two slopes in the town; **Le Savoy**, behind the massive Club Med building, and **Les Planards**, near the train station. Both are beginner-friendly areas but have variable snow due to their low altitude (1035m). Luckily, they are supported by extensive snow-making facilities.

In terms of piste length, official numbers give 155km of groomed trails. This pales in comparison with the super-resorts of the Alps (Espace Killy, Paradiski, Portes du Soleil etc) but bear in mind the pistes in Chamonix, as well as being fun in their own right, are also there to provide access to the immense off-piste the area has to offer.

Chamonix's lift system feels archaic when compared to some resorts. Creaky cable cars and fixed-cable chairlifts prevail, which cause plenty of bottlenecks on busy days. However, in fairness, the Compagnie du Mont Blanc are in the middle of a programme to upgrade the tired lift infrastructure.

Le Brévent

Chances are that Brévent will be the first resort that you ski; it's located right in town, so is by far the easiest to get to on the first morning of your trip. Most people

On the piste

catch the draglift from behind Club Med to get to the fast Planpraz gondola, which was new for winter 2008-9. South-facing Brévent is a real sun-trap, so remember to take your sunscreen.

> ### Where to?
>
> **Blue sky and fresh powder:** choose La Flégère and escape the long lift lines and powder-mania of Les Grands Montets
>
> **Snowy:** head to Vallorcine and ski the tree-lined runs from the Tête de Balme chair down to Vallorcine village
>
> **Windy:** go to Les Houches, which is lower and more sheltered than the rest of the valley
>
> **High rain line:** go to Les Grands Montets and ski Herse and Grands Montets to stay in the snow. Download in the Lognan cable car once you're finished
>
> **After dark:** should the urge for a moonlight slide prove irresistible, the Tourchet draglift and piste in Les Houches (in the centre of the village) are open on Thursday evenings, normally until 9pm (depending on demand). There's also a full moon descent of the Vallée Blanche (p.115).

The area is connected to La Flégère via a short cable car. The **Les Nants** homerun, which links the resort back to Chamonix, is a lovely piste when open; check before you commit. If it's closed, you'll have to take the Planpraz gondola down, perhaps after you've enjoyed a tipple in the neighbouring Bergerie mountain restaurant (p.89).

La Flégère

Accessed via cable car from the quiet little hamlet of Les Praz, just a short ride on the local bus from Chamonix itself, La Flégère is an excellent mountain for those intermediates just getting a taste of the steep runs found in the valley. The reds off the fast Index chair

are sensational, although for longer pistes you'll need to ride the draglift of the Floria. Watch out as it jerks you away from a standing stop... and take care on the dog-leg left halfway up. Again, a ski-out homerun back to Les Praz is open in good snow conditions, otherwise you'll be taking the cable car down. This can get busy, so another option is to catch the Liaison cable car back to Brévent and then download on the faster gondola.

Le Tour

The horseshoe bowl of Le Tour offers spectacular views down the valley. It's accessed from the village of the same name at 1462m. However, the train station is quite a way away from the town itself, so if you're travelling around by train, consider heading to Vallorcine, just over the back of Le Tour; the station sits right next to the lift. Alternatively, Le Tour is serviced by the local bus that leaves all of the Chamonix stops regularly.

However, back on the frontside, from the Le Tour bottom station you'll take a gondola to mid-station, then a chair to the top. The sunny pistes at Le Tour are quiet in the week, and as they're wide and not too steep they're ideal for beginners and improving intermediates. However it can get busy on weekends and in the holiday times, so think about traversing around via the **Liaison Balme** piste to the back side of the mountain, and the runs down to Vallorcine village. They're a lot quieter and often have better snow thanks to the shade.

Les Grands Montets

The Grands Montets is the highest 'resort' in Chamonix, soaring to a dizzying 3275m at the top of the viewing platform. It frequently has the best snow of all the ski areas and, since it doesn't get much sun, the snow stays good for days after a dump. The base station is served by the regular bus from Chamonix and the Argentière train station is less than five minutes' walk away; a good thing too, since Grands Montets is by far the most popular area to ski. It's laid out as a series of bowls cut into the side of a high peak, all sitting below the glaciers which funnel down off the Petite Aiguille Verte high above.

Les Houches

Chamonix's sister resort, at the south-west end of the valley, is less steep than the other resorts in the valley. It's lower in altitude, and nearly all below treeline, so it's a pretty, quiet and sheltered little place. Families and beginners make up the majority of the resort's visitors, and fill the streets of the mini base village. This all changes when the other Chamonix ski areas are closed due to wind, at which point Les Houches becomes extremely busy.

Getting on the slopes

Since Chamonix is a functioning town slotted around a number of different ski areas, getting to the slopes is like commuting to work; it has to be done, and with a little planning is relatively painless. Despite rumours to the contrary, the notable lack of ski in, ski out accommodation doesn't have to ruin your holiday.

Reserving cabins

Because the highest lifts in Chamonix are the ones everybody wants to get on, the queues get fairly intense, especially just after fresh snow has fallen. Thankfully, if you're smart and in the know, you can avoid the worst of the lift lines for Les Grands Montets and the Aiguille du Midi. As long as you've already bought your Mont-Blanc Unlimited lift pass (available months in advance from **compagniedumontblanc.com**) just log onto the same website and hit one of the big 'reserve' buttons. You can book from seven days to 24hrs in advance, and by printing your reservation you can skip the long queues and just hop on.

The Mont-Blanc Express

Chamonix's red and white train winds through the valley every hour on its way from Le Fayet to Le Châtelard. Travel is free from Servoz to Vallorcine using a Carte d'Hôte, which you can get (for free) from your accommodation provider. Get off the train at Chamonix for Brévent; Les Praz for Flégère; Argentière for Les Grands Montets and Vallorcine for Le Tour. If you are heading to Le Tour remember you can get off at Montroc, but you'll have to wait for a bus to take you a kilometre up the hill to the lift. You'll find Chamonix station on Avenue de la Gare, right in the centre of Chamonix, opposite Chambre Neuf. Follow the numerous signs for 'Gare' (station).

Chamonix bus

During the ski season the bus network in the valley is convenient and extensive (though before December and after March it's restricted to one per hour). However, the downside is that buses are frequently late and often packed with skiers. Timetables are available from the tourist office and the reception of most hotels.

If you decide to drive, there is plenty of free parking at all the resorts except for Brévent, which charges €1 per day.

Mad Dog Ski Chamonix

Piste map

Chamonix's piste map isn't the easiest in the world to follow; lots of different areas and lots of different aspects make a designer's nightmare! Thankfully the signage once on the piste is very clear. The important thing to remember is that only the resorts of Brévent and La Flégère are linked. Elsewhere, bus or train connections are necessary if you want to move between different areas.

The best map is the official Compagnie du Mont Blanc map, available for free at all of the ski area base stations or from the town centre tourist office.

Beginners

It's true that Chamonix offers a particularly unique challenge for the first-time skier or rider; the geography of this place means there's a lot more steep terrain than beginner slopes – thus the learning curve is fairly steep too. Early intermediates will have plenty to do here, though absolute beginners are likely to find more fun, along with a more extensive area to explore, in the neighbouring resorts of Megève and Les Contamines.

First-timers to winter sports will enjoy the relaxed atmosphere of the beginner ski area at Les Planards, just behind the train station. From the new 4-man chair, follow the gently meandering **Piste Bleu** run around the back, through the woods to get some beautiful views over the valley.

Le Tour, Chamonix's most mellow resort, has some excellent beginner terrain. But the **Forêt Verte** shines as a particular highlight, with jaw-dropping views and few people. Though classified as a blue run, as it's narrow in a couple of places, the trail is lovely. From the top of the Vallorcine gondola, take the **Esserts** run as it winds through the woods, then stay high and left as the Tête de Balme chair comes into sight. Cruise down the path through the forest, admiring the immense Emosson Dam on the other side, to the high village of Vallorcine.

On the piste

maddogski.com

35

Intermediates

Intermediate skiers will certainly enjoy the challenge Chamonix offers; the resort's 'experts only' reputation is primarily because of the extensive ski mountaineering and off-piste access. Fortunately, there are also plenty of red and blue runs to cruise.

The Chamois at Brévent is a local favourite. A real sun-trap, receiving loads of light through the course of the day, the altitude means that the snow conditions are good more often than not. From the Cornu chair, follow the run and curve back under the lift, then head down, looking out for the turning to the right. This is where the trail narrows, cutting beneath the Chamois bowl off-piste area. The banked corners and swooping zig-zag turns are fun on skis or a board – it's why this run is considered the natural 'boardercross' track of Chamonix.

Les Houches has some excellent terrain for more accomplished skiers, although the good stuff can be pretty hard to find. Our favourite trail is the tucked-away **Fontaines** that runs from the top of the Kandahar chair through the woods to the bottom of the Crozat chair. It's hugely atmospheric, feeling almost like a nature trail, and the sight of Megève, Les Contamines and St Gervais in the distance, with the whole of the Arve valley laid out in the foreground, is quite something.

Advanced

Les Grands Montets is one of the finest playgrounds in the world for advanced skiers. Head up the Top, the highest cable car there, and walk down the stairs to the flattish plateau below the Aiguille Verte, the white dome that soars up nearly 1000m above you. At the bottom of the stairs, turn left and follow the steep **Pylones**, cutting through the moguls that often form on the steeper sections. Ignore the turn-off to the left, staying on the **Point de Vue**, flying down the trail with the stupendous views over the Argentière glacier over your right shoulder and the dizzying Grand Mur over your left.

At La Flégère, the Lachanel bowl is often missed by skiers, due to its hard-to-read signage. Take the high-speed Index chairlift to the top station, turn left off the chair, passing in the low part of the ridgeline to open up the Lachanel. Although officially a red run, **Lachanel** is very steep and offers some excellent possibilities for riding the open-jaw-like ridges that soar out of the snow on either side of the markers. In good snow years there's an off-piste itinerary that allows skiers to head straight down to Les Praz, under the Liaison, from here. If you don't know the way, play safe and cruise down to the Evettes chair.

If all this sounds complicated, a great option is to hire a guide (p.43). They can help you orientate yourself and will always know which runs have the best snow.

Off-piste

Chamonix is doubtless the prime destination for off-piste skiers in the Alps. It's important to remember that the area is fairly unusual in that a lot of its off-piste skiing is on glaciers. These constantly changing ice megaliths are home to many dangers, both from above (serac falls) and from below (invisible crevasses beneath the snow). Whatever your skiing ability, we recommend booking a mountain guide (p.43) to ensure your safety in this hostile, high-mountain environment... which is often where you'll find the best conditions!

Les Grands Montets

Les Grands Montets offers a huge amount of lift-accessed vertical drop in optimum snow conditions, setting off from the Grands Montets and Pendant glaciers. The world up around the glaciers of this area is very different from other off-piste areas. The harnesses, rope and heavy-duty rescue gear carried by every off-piste skier up here are worn for a reason.

The Lavancher bowl, accessed from the Bochard gondola at Grands Montets, is a fresh-tracks favourite amongst locals, and drops you out at the Pendant Retour chair. Alternately, there's a route down to the village of Lavancher itself, down what is a zig-zaggy footpath in the summer.

Since the majority of the off-piste in Chamonix is above

On the piste

Avalanche!

Whilst Chamonix has a number of explosive and compressed-air systems to prevent avalanches, the danger cannot be completely averted and every year people die on the mountain.

Speed is of the essence if you are caught in an avalanche; if the victim is alive after the initial impact there is an 80% chance of survival if rescued in the first 12 minutes, after 15 minutes the probability of a successful rescue drops dramatically. Your best chance of survival is to be rescued by someone in your own group.
A transceiver, shovel and probe are essential kit for off-piste skiing, along with the knowledge of how to use them. Although manufacturers claim that mobile phones cause only minimum interference with transceiver signals, it is also recommended that you switch your mobile off whilst off-piste.

The daily avalanche risk is shown clearly with flags and ratings on a scale of 1-5 throughout the ski area. If in doubt, ask a piste security employee.

Avalanche warning flags

Yellow	Black/yellow chequered flag	Black flag
Level 1-2	Level 3-4	Level 5
Limited risk	High risk	Very high risk

See **meteofrance.com** for the daily avalanche bulletin. You'll also find it posted outside the Maison de la Montagne, opposite the tourist office.

Safety

Most accidents are caused by collisions; it is relatively easy for adults to achieve speeds of over 50kph, and even children can quite easily reach 45kph. Be aware of others around you and follow the piste rules.

1. Respect – do not endanger or prejudice the safety of others

2. Control – ski in control, adapting your speed and manner to ability, conditions and traffic. Give way to slower skiers

3. Choice of route – the skier who is further up the slope must choose his route so he does not endanger the skiers below

4. Overtaking – allowed left or right, above or below but always leave sufficient space for the overtaken skier

5. Entering and starting a run – look both up and down the piste before you head off

6. Stopping on the piste – avoid stopping at narrow or low visibility areas. Always stop at the edge of the piste rather than in the middle and make sure that you can be easily seen by approaching skiers

7. Climbing – if you have to walk up or down the piste, do so at the edge and ensure neither you nor your equipment are a danger to anyone else

8. Signs and markings – respect the information given about pistes and the weather

9. Accidents – if you witness an accident, you must give assistance, particularly by alerting piste security

10. Identification – if you are involved in or witness an accident, you must provide your identity to piste security if requested

The International Ski Federation (FIS) Code of Conduct

On the piste

maddogski.com

tree-line, it can get disorientating in bad weather. When the clouds come in, people head to the Magic Forest – a lovely area of cliffs and gullies in the pine forest next to the Plan Roujon chairlift.

Le Brévent

Brévent's off-piste is amazing, particularly so early in the morning, before the sun gets over the Aiguille du Midi and starts to thicken and melt the snow. No glaciers here, so avalanche is the primary hazard of which to be aware. Of all the lines, the L'ENSA couloir is the best known – it's the dog-leg to the looker's left of the Brévent top station when viewed from Planpraz. A rappel is often required into the line as the top is so steep, it rarely has enough snow on it to ski. Further round the Brévent bowl is the Payot area, another great steep-skiing destination, with tree-lined chutes that empty out into the same exit as the L'ENSA.

You'll often hear of locals talking of the Hotel Face slopes, which are above the main ski area of Brévent and accessed via a traverse from the **Charles Bozon** run (under the left-hand rope when the piste takes its first big right-hand turn). There are plenty of options here, as well as the opportunity for getting lost or stranded above a cliff band; so take care and go with a guide. A better idea for those new to off-piste skiing could be the Chamois bowl, reached via a traverse in the direction of Chamonix from the top of the Col Cornu chair. There's a little arête to climb before you get into the bowl itself. Equally, the Charlanon bowl, on the other side of the Cornu chair, is a lot of fun and requires less commitment.

La Flégère

Riding off-piste at La Flégère is very popular in Chamonix – it is unglaciated, requiring fewer emergency skills than the Grands Montets or Aguille du Midi runs. The gullies of the Floria area are excellent, almost like natural halfpipes. With a deep coat of powder on, this terrain is brilliant fun. From the top of the Floria drag lift, make your way a few metres down the **Floria** piste, before peeling off to the right and negotiating your way down the rollers back to the bottom of the Trappe chairlift.

Le Tour

Being the shallowest resort in the valley doesn't necessarily mean that the off-piste runs are the same. In fact, the back bowls of Le Tour are of incredibly high standard – the only negative is their aspect, which makes them prone to wind-loading and subsequently high avalanche risk. They merit care and respect when being skied. Access is via the Tête de Balme chairlift on the back side of Le Tour; drop under the chairlift and cut to skier's right to access the terrain. The exits – which take you back to the bottom of the chair – are easy to miss and it's a long slog through dense forest if you end up going the wrong way.

Vallée Blanche

Whilst Grands Montets is the favourite resort for off-piste skiing, the Aiguille du Midi cable car is a Chamonix phenomenon. Named after the towering spire that sits above the town at 3842m, the two-stage cable car shoots up to the high point to bring sightseers and thrillseekers alike right up into the high country. Though the Pré du Rocher off-piste descents down the couloirs from mid-station back to town are great in the right snow conditions, people go up to the Aiguille du Midi to ski the world-famous Vallée Blanche. The most important thing to remember is that, whatever you may hear, the Vallée Blanche is not a piste. Far from it; inexperienced skiers and riders die up here every year. The dangers are many and prevalent, from serac fall, acute mountain sickness, hidden crevasses, snow bridge collapses, avalanches... the list goes on.

Whilst there are many ways to do yourself harm on the routes from the Aiguille, there are also many ways to have the most memorable ski descent of your life. Play it safe and get a high mountain guide to show you the ski-movie scenery of the Grands,

Moyen and Petit Envers; the Vrai Vallée; the Droit du Rognan, as well as the classic Vallée Blanche. The flat section at the bottom of the glacier is a pain for tired snowboarders, especially late in the season or even late in the day – telescopic poles to 'punt' yourself along with are a great help. If you're not sure if you're good enough don't panic; if you can confidently ski a pisted red run, you'll be fine with a guide.

Once at the end of the epic adventure, skis come off for a 20 minute walk up to the Montenvers gondola before settling into the Montenvers rack-and-pinion train for the ride down to Chamonix. Even if there's enough snow to ski back to town, this is by far the most popular way of getting down; the run-out back to Chamonix follows a narrow footpath and is not great skiing.

Heli-skiing

For environmental reasons, heli-skiing is not permitted in France. However, Chamonix has the advantage of being the meeting point of the French, Italian and Swiss borders, so it's reasonably easy to find a willing guide agency who will take you across the border, where heli drops are legal.

The Trient glacier is one of the most popular destinations. For agencies to contact, see the Mountain guides section to the right.

Mountain guides

If you're wondering whether to book a guide or not, the answer is 'yes'. Not only will the guide make you safer, they'll lead you to the best snow in places you wouldn't find alone.

These are the most popular guides amongst English-speaking visitors. The cost is reduced the bigger your group, up to a general maximum of six per guide. If you're in a group of four, expect to pay around €50 per person for a guided lap of the Vallée Blanche, whereas private day rates for guides start from €300 per day.

Chamex
Argentière
t +33 (0)4 50 54 09 36
w chamex.com

Evolution 2
Chamonix
t +33 (0)4 50 55 90 22
w evolution2-chamonix.com

Yak & Yeti
Chamonix
t + 33 (0)4 50 53 53 67
w yak-yeti.com

In addition to the agencies, these private guides come highly recommended for off-piste skiing in Chamonix. They are British, fully qualified and sometimes cheaper than the agencies.

Andy Perkins
t +33 (0)4 50 54 33 86
w andypmountainguide.com

Dream Guides
w dream-guides.com
e info@dream-guides.com

Stuart Macdonald
w stuartmacdonald.org
e info@stuartmacdonald.org

Snowboarders

Chamonix has a reputation as being friendlier to skiers than boarders. On piste however, that reputation isn't really deserved. Because of the steepness of the geography, there are actually far fewer cat tracks and flat spots than in other resorts. There's a snowpark at Les Grands Montets and in the same area you'll find the sweeping banked turns and tabletop launches of the boardercross course.

Off-piste, things change. Lots of the best powder runs are accessed by long traverses, often above steep and rocky terrain. Boarders are best waiting for a skier to put the traverse in first, then following the laid track. Also, often lamented in Chamonix is the lack of trees (due to the steepness of the slopes) and the height of the mountains. Although there are several excellent tree runs to be found, the extent of them is nothing like the glades of Verbier, Val d'Isère or Morzine.

Terrain parks

The freestyle scene in Chamonix remains in its infancy; jumps aren't really what people come here to ride. The first snowpark, designed by Grenoble-based pro park shapers HO5, was put in above Lognan at Les Grands Montets for winter 2005/6. Every year the park has grown in length and scope, and now encompasses several lines of jumps for different ability levels. Rails are the weak point; if you fancy riding rails, you're probably better off checking out the small snow park under the "Schuss des Dames" chair on the Bellevue side of Les Houches, which has better quality jibs, including c-boxes and rainbow rails.

Alternately, after a heavy snowfall there are often groups of locals setting up street-rails around the town itself. The area behind the Casino is a favourite spot for unofficial rail action.

Cross-country

Although Chamonix is primarily known as a destination for Alpine skiing, cross-country is very popular here for long-term aficionados, people wanting to maintain their cardiac fitness during the winter months, or for skiers looking for a change. The central hub for cross-country skiing is the trailhead just opposite MBC (p.86), where there's an enormous Club des Sports building. The folks there are very helpful about conditions on the 42km of trails.

As for the routes, there are several green, blue and red trails which wind up from the Les Bois area, popping out at the top of the valley just before Argentière. Beware some savage climbs.

maddogski.com

Les Houches offers some gentler cross-country terrain at altitude; there's a 4.2km track around the plateau at the top of the Prarion gondola. Trail use is free, but you'll need a pass for the gondola to get up there. Return pedestrian lift passes are available for €9.90.

Equipment can be hired in Chamonix town centre:

Ravanel & Co General Store
t + 33 (0)4 50 53 02 49
w ravanel-sportshop.com
Galerie Alpina, Place du Mt-Blanc.

Lift passes

The Compagnie du Mont Blanc changes their lift pass options frequently, making it tricky to plan ahead. In particular in the village of Les Houches, which is partly run by the Compagnie du Mont Blanc (Prarion side) and partly by a local company called SEPP (Bellevue side). Every year the two companies struggle to agree on access rights for passholders of the two areas.

Similarly, up in Chamonix, two types of passes exist at the time of going to press. The 'Chamonix Le Pass' option is aimed at the intermediate or budget-conscious skier, and allows access to the entire valley excluding Les Houches, the top lift at Les Grands Montets, the Aiguille du Midi, the Tramway du Mont Blanc and the Montenvers cog railway.

Meanwhile, the 'Mont Blanc Unlimited' option targets freeriders and sightseers alike, providing access to everything at greater expense. Courmayeur is also included in the Unlimited pass,

Adult lift pass prices

Chamonix Le Pass*
1 day	€38.50
6 days	€192
7 days	€215

Mont Blanc Unlimited
1 day	€48.50
6 days	€235
7 days	€265

* can be upgraded to Mont Blanc Unlimited for around €20 a day.

with a free return bus trip or reduced-price Mont Blanc Tunnel return tickets to get you there. Holders of Chamonix Le Pass can upgrade to the Mont Blanc Unlimited for around €20 a day.

The result is that you have to do some maths to work out which pass provides value for you. Most visitors seem to take the Chamonix Le Pass, upgrading as necessary, often squeezing the Grands Montets top lift freeriding and Vallée Blanche into one thrill-filled day to save a few bucks. If you don't want the stress of it and want maximum flexibility, and don't mind paying a bit extra, get the Mont Blanc Unlimited. See **compagniedumontblanc.com** for more details.

Weather

As with any mountain town, Chamonix has fairly unpredictable weather that can change rapidly. Generally, the weather comes into town from the direction of Mont Blanc and heads north-west. Slopes with this aspect are vulnerable to cornicing and wind loading – you'll see particular evidence of this in the Vallorcine area, where the avalanche risk is always high even long after a snowfall.

In the valley it's not uncommon to see storm systems getting stuck in the mountains, with thickish banks of cloud

maddogski.com

caught hanging above the valley floor. From the window in the morning it looks like the day will be horrible, but once you're above the cloud blanket layer it is often glorious sunshine. Keep an eye on the weather report in English at **chamonix-meteo.com** and **maddogski.com**.

Ski and snowboard schools

The two main schools in Chamonix are the **ESF** and **Evolution 2**; the former being a classic French ski school, the latter a smaller company with a more progressive teaching approach. Recently, a small number of boutique British-led schools have come into existence, which specialise in certain disciplines.

All Mountain Performance
t +33 (0)6 87 69 83 86
w allmountainperformance.com
Mark Gear is based in Les Houches but he and his team organise ski-only teaching sessions all over the valley. Their philosophy is to use straightforward coaching techniques and to make the most of the valley's off-piste terrain as a teaching tool. The five instructors are all lifelong skiers and English-speaking, which has made this excellent little ski school popular with the British crowd. Half a day of private tuition for two people costs around €230.

ESF
t +33 (0)4 50 53 22 57
w esfchamonix.com
Place de l'eglise.
The Ecole de Ski Francaise are in every resort in the French Alps,

and their red-jacketed moniteurs epitomise every ski instructor cliché in the book. The company's size naturally means the service is less personal, and the product more standardised, though this also means they have good availability pretty much all season long. Half a day of private tuition for two people costs around €230.

Evolution 2

t +33 (0)4 50 55 90 22
w evolution2-chamonix.com
A mini-ESF, Evo 2 is a small, friendly ski school with plenty of full-time instructors, most of whom speak English (though do request an English-speaking instructor when you book). Evolution 2 is just as good for snowboard lessons and has a dedicated 'Panda Club' which takes care of kids starting out in snowsports. Half a day of private tuition for two people costs around €175.

McNab

t +44 141 416 3828
w mcnabsnowboarding.com
Neil NcNab is a former British Snowboard Champion. He's a mountain guide, a passionate snowboarder and wrote the British book of snowboard instruction. Neil and his crew run courses and private lessons which are booked up months in advance; if you're a snowboarder and you want to get better, this is the man to call.

Equipment hire

When it comes to hiring gear there's plenty of choice in Chamonix; for those on a tight budget to those wanting to spend a little more on top-end snow sports gear. You'll find unusual items too, thanks to the huge diversity of sports stores; splitboards, trekking skis, snowshoes, ice-climbing gear, transceivers, reverse-camber skis and boards... it really is a shopaholics paradise.

Otavalo

t +33 (0)4 50 53 02 17
w otavalo-chamonix.com
163 Rue Vallot.
When telemarkers come to town they head straight to Otavalo for their gear. Telemarking, the free-heel version of Alpine skiing,

On the piste

maddogski.com

has quite a following in Chamonix, with many visitors electing to 'give it a go' for a day (normally towards the end of their holiday!). As one of the leading tele shops in Western Europe, Otavalo is full of friendly advice.

Pro Ski
t +33 (0)4 50 53 58 92
w proskimontagne.com
178-220 Avenue Michel Croz.
This Rossignol pro shop is generally considered the place to go for ski rental in town. Located a stone's throw from the train station, from the outside it blends in to the array of other shops; however, once inside you'll realise that the warm welcome and the quality of the gear make it stand out.

Snell Sports
t +33 (0)4 50 53 02 17
w cham3s.com
104 Rue du Docteur Paccard.
A visit to Chamonix is not complete without stopping by Snell Sports, which offers prime wallet-emptying potential with a Tesco-sized floorspace full of outdoor kit. Although the skis and boards here fall into the 'average' category, the mountaineering equipment for hire is top notch. Recommended particularly for Vallée Blanche daytrippers who need to sort themselves out crampons, a harness and avalanche gear for the day.

Technique Extreme
t +33 (0)4 50 53 63 14
w technique-extreme.com
200 Avenue de l'Aiguille du Midi.
Whilst the blinged-up mountaineering brigade might view Technique Extreme as the Primark of the mountains, there's no denying they're cheap. If you want the lowest cost gear in town, you've found the right place.

Zero G
t + 33 (0)4 50 53 01 01
w zerogchx.com
90 Ravanel le Rouge.
A snowboard-only shop that's been in Chamonix for over twenty years and is one of the last remaining 'core' shops in the Alps. Zero G are known for their decent rental equipment; capstrap-only bindings, Burton & Vans boots and a full Demo House of gear.

Piste rankings

Skiers the world over are greeted by piste maps with a rainbow of different coloured trails criss-crossing the mountain. In the US, double-, or even triple-, black diamonds are not uncommon, whilst over here red runs mystify any non-European. Only one thing remains constant worldwide; the easier trails don't mean 'easy', they mean 'easier'. A black run in Resort A might be very tricky for that resort, whereas anyone used to Resort B will find it a walk in the park. Owing to the extreme terrain of Chamonix, many visitors stick to intermediate runs for the first few days until they're ready for the unique challenges of the black runs of the valley. People often say that a red run here is a black anywhere else.

You can only have real in-depth knowledge if you live and ski all the runs regularly. To help you, our researchers have ranked the main red and black pistes using a star rating (* = easier and *** = more challenging).

Factors such as gradient, width, grooming and skier traffic have been taken into account, as well as whether the slope is north- or south-facing.

Pistes are listed in alphabetical order by ski area; reds first, then blacks.

maddogski.com

Piste	Comments
Les Grands Montets red pistes	
Bochard*	The most popular run at the resort is full of side hits for freestylers and wide, shallow-angle schusses for carvers.
Combes**	This long run is a real thigh-burner late in the day after it's had a lot of skier traffic, but on cold mornings is perfect for ripping up the freshly-pisted surface.
Pierre à Ric**	The home-run back down to valley level is best skied in the morning; by 2pm it's mogul hell, filled with tired, zig-zagging skiers trying to get home in one piece. Take the Lognan cable car down instead.
Les Grands Montets black pistes	
Blanchots***	Steep and usually mogul-filled.
Chamois*	Wide open, fast, flowing run full of corner drop-offs and rollers to catch some air.
Point de Vue*	A steep start up on the glacier, with breathtaking views over the Argentière basin.
Pylônes**	Normally unpisted, good in fresh snow but otherwise rutted and hard going.
Remuaz*	Steep and often mogully; best ridden in slushy snow on March and April afternoons.

Piste	Comments
Balme (Le Tour) red pistes	
Aiguillette*	A dead-straight downhill parallel to the drag lift of the same name. Above tree-line so avoid in bad weather... or if you don't like an audience to your skiing.
Alpages*	Steep at the top, this piste is full of good views over the Chamonix valley. Mind out for the very steep depressions just off to the left of the run.
Belle-Place**	Straight, wide open and undulating between flatter and steeper gradients with some interesting depressions – don't fall at the bottom of one! Access to the back bowls (p.41).
Caisets*	The home run, which was redesigned for 2008/9 is now wider, with fewer choke-points and steep sections. Thankfully there's still plenty of time to get some speed up for the final schuss back to the Charamillon gondola base.
Châtelet**	Snowboarders won't appreciate the flattish top section but, once through that, the Châtelet piste skirts the cliffs of the Vormaine bowl and offers a wonderful natural playground of gullies and side-hits.
Ecuries*	Winds between the gully-like natural halfpipe watercourses of the Le Tour frontside; a great way for the intermediate skier to start the day.

maddogski.com

Piste	Comments
Brévent red pistes	
Chamois**	The obvious way down from the Cornu chair often becomes mogully, so those in the know take the first right turn and tackle the fast traverses, tabletops and banked bends of Brévent's unofficial, natural boardercross track.
La Charlanon***	Even though it's a red, it's not a run for the faint of heart; steep at the top and narrow at the bottom, the run is brilliant in fresh snow but quite a challenge in more brittle conditions.
Cornu*	A wide, popular ski with great views over the Mont Blanc Massif.

Piste	Comments
Brévent black pistes	
Charles Bozon**	The Hotel Face is accessed from the turn-off under the ropes of the third bend of this long, fast piste named for a Chamonix racer. The steepness means that you lose so much height so fast that your ears pop from the pressure change as you sprint down the winding, narrow, steep run.
Nants*	The Brévent home-run is only open when the snow line is low enough; the piste is resonably easy for a black run, with banked corners and plenty of places to stop for a rest at the side. Beware the very long, very flat run-out before the Savoy beginner's area right at the bottom.
Variante*	The Variante offers a slower, less challenging ski than the Bozon, with less skier traffic and a wider piste.
Variante Charlanon*	Often sun-soaked, the snow here gets lumpy pretty quickly, rendering it all but unskiable apart from in the early mornings.

maddogski.com

Piste	Comments
Flégère red pistes	
Crochues**	A wide, swinging piste with few people and spectacular views over the Mer de Glace glacier on the other side of the valley.
Lachenal*	A charming secret red run ignored by most visitors as they turn right (away) at the top of the Index chair. Instead, head left and through the rocky ridge to open up the stunning views, cruisy turns and normally excellent snow of this overlooked piste.
Pylônes**	The busiest route down from the Index chair has plenty of rollers and fast steep sections, whilst not being too challenging for the intermediate-level skier. Something for everyone.
Flégère black pistes	
Floria***	A long, steep route which is unpisted most of the time.
Pic Janvier***	This steep, ungroomed route from the top of the Index chair is very hard work in all but the deepest, freshest snow.
Praz**	The Flégère home-run is not as much fun as the Brévent equivalent; only consider it if you're staying in Les Praz, otherwise get the Liaison cable car back to Brévent and ski the Nants home-run down.

Piste	Comments
Les Houches red pistes	
Bellevue*	Gentler than Grands Bois, and not as fast.
Col de Voza*	Very wide – but uneven to skier's right. One of the top priorities for the piste-bashers so often well groomed.
Fontaines**	Cruisy run which misses most of the resort's skier traffic; beautiful views over Passy and the lower Arve valley.
Grands Bois**	Wide, treelined, steep and straight. Excellent in fresh snow.
Mur des Epines*	The long, meandering alternative way down to the Verte des Houches.
Plancerts*	Fast but relatively low-angle run with lots of ups and downs.
Plan du Crêt*	Offers great tree-skiing in good snow conditions.
Stade*	A wide, sweeping red with plenty of rollers to catch air off.
Table d'Orientation*	Very similar to Stade, just the other side of the trees.

Piste	Comments
Les Houches black pistes	
Schuss des Dames*	Steep, short, rarely pisted so often mogulled.
Verte des Houches**	Les Houches' classic plunging Alpine downhill racetrack; long and fast.

Lift types

Lifts are shown with symbols for the lift type:

Cable car
Chairlift
T-bar/drag
Gondola

Piste names appear in their classified colour.

Day trips

There are lots of great routes to explore Chamonix and the surrounding area; here are two of our favourites. You can download more from **maddogski.com**.

Aim to start these trips around 8.30am, meaning you will finish around 2.30pm. Suggested places to stop for lunch are included in the itineraries. Timings are based on the pace of a competent red-run skier and assume good conditions and average lift queues. Allow additional time if you are skiing more slowly or during weekends and holidays, when the resort is busier. Our researchers have worked hard to make these itineraries as accurate as possible. However pistes and routes can change from season to season so please take a piste map with you in case anything is unclear.

The sun circuit

This tour starts at the Planpraz gondola. To get there, walk up the Mollard hill from Chamonix town. You'll need a Chamonix Le Pass lift ticket.

Lift	Comments
Planpraz	Enjoy the nine minute ride up to 2000m. Look out the back of the gondola for magnificent views of the sun rising up over the Mont Blanc Massif.
Brévent	Head up to 2525m – the Brévent itself. Spot extreme skiers in the Bellin couloir below and take in the view over the town. From the top you can see Flaine to the north-west, just a couple of miles away as the crow flies. Head down **Charles Bozon**, which isn't all that bad, and as you start to near the chairlifts and restaurants, stick left onto Blanchots. Follow this wide, empty piste all the way down to the Cornu chair.
Cornu	From the top, follow Cornu down, turning quickly right onto the narrow and windy variant of Chamois – this is Chamonix's unofficial boardercross circuit, but skiers also enjoy the rollers and raised corners of this narrow, windy piste until getting back to the Cornu chair.
Cornu	Climb onto the Cornu once again, and this time take Charlanon (straight on at the top). After the first long, wide, plunging section, keep to the left on Tétras as you go past the top of the Charlanon chair, and follow signs for the Liaison.

maddogski.com

Lift	Comments
Liaison	This whisks you above the cliffs of the Lachanél bowl to La Flégère; click your skis on for the short descent to the Evettes chair, which will take you back up through the forest.
Evettes	From the top, follow the short blue piste down towards mid-station.
Lunch	There's a lovely sundeck here, with a booth selling good (though a little pricey) coffee and sandwiches. Great for a quick lunch stop – and if you've brought a picnic, tuck in.

Lift	Comments
Index	This 8-man lift will drop you off at 2396m. From here, take **Pylônes** as it snakes back down to mid-station; the run follows the lift practically the whole way. Once back at mid-station, hop back on the same lift.
Index	This time take a left off the chair, through the small gap in the rocks to **Lachanél**. This one is a beauty in the early-afternoon sunshine, with spectacular views across to the Grandes Jorasses. The run will bring you out at the Index again, which you should take for a third time.
Index	This time turn right at the top and traverse above the hut to the Floria draglift.
Floria	The rickety old surface tow will trundle you up to the highest point of the resort, from which you should take **Crochues** all the way down to the bottom of the Trappe chair.
Trappe	From the top of the Trappe it's just a short ski back to mid-station, from which you can take the Praz homerun down to the village of the same name to get the bus back to Chamonix. If the homerun is shut, make your way back to Brévent via the Liaison cable car.

The heights & sights of Argentière

You'll need the Mont Blanc Unlimited lift pass to complete this day trip. Start the day by taking the train to Vallorcine station (free with the Carte d'Hôte pass that your hotel or chalet will give you). The Vallorcine gondola is just by the train station.

Lift	Comments
Vallorcine	From the gondola, head down the tree-lined, low-angle **Esserts** run to the Tête de Balme chairlift.
Tête de Balme	Take the **Belle Place** – a tremendously fast, open, confidence-building red – back down to the same chairlift, and go up again.
Tête de Balme	This time cut left at the top, onto the **Alpages** trail. You're heading for the draglift you can see off to the right in the distance.
Aiguillette	Head up to the Posettes peak at nearly 2200m. Head down **Posettes**, then turn right onto **Retour Charamillon** to bring you to the mid-station of Le Tour.
Lunch	There's a restaurant here, the Chalet de Charamillon; whilst the à-la-carte food is overpriced, the sandwich deals are good value, and the sun-terrace makes a lovely setting for lunch.
Autannes	Turn right at the top, onto **Châtelet**, which will take you back down to mid-station. Keep going down on **Caisets**, which takes you below the Charamillon gondola to the bottom of Le Tour. Catch the bus (the bus stop is on the bridge) for the 10-minute journey to Les Grands Montets, getting off after passing through Argentière and the Grands Montets car park; the bus stops right next to the Lognan cable car station.

maddogski.com

Lift	Comments
Lognan	Exit at mid-station then transfer onto the Bochard gondola.
Bochard	It's a quick journey up to 2765m. Now ski down the first section of Bochard, quickly turning left onto **Chamois** which will take you into Pendant Bowl. Fork left onto the **Chamois-Arolles** link, then cruise down the blue Arolles itself until you arrive at the Retour-Pendant chairlift.
Retour-Pendant	From the top take **Marmottons** back to mid-station and pick up the Grands Montets cable car.
Grands Montets	Get ready for an enormous 2000m of vertical in one run. Walk down the steps from the Grands Montets arrival station to the piste and enjoy the incredible views of the Argentière basin. Take the **Point de Vue** which snakes down the side of the Argentière glacier. It's a beautiful run; take your time, because before you know it you're back at Lognan. Turn right just before the cable car station, onto Pierre à Ric, for the last 700m of vertical until you hit the base station of Grands Montets. From here, use your Carte d'Hôte to get the free bus back to Chamonix (25 minutes).

Where to find the best **food and drink**, from pizzas and local specialities to luxurious restaurants.

What you'll find in this chapter

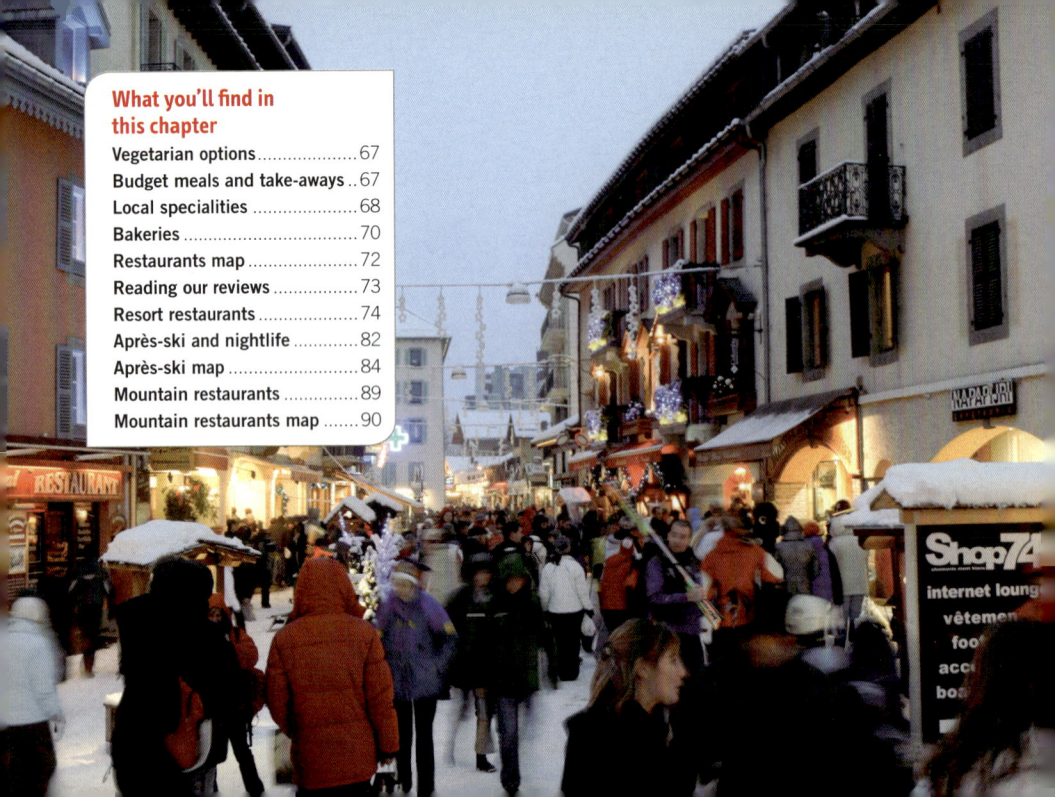

Vegetarian options	67
Budget meals and take-aways	67
Local specialities	68
Bakeries	70
Restaurants map	72
Reading our reviews	73
Resort restaurants	74
Après-ski and nightlife	82
Après-ski map	84
Mountain restaurants	89
Mountain restaurants map	90

Food and drink

Chamonix is a town in its own right, not just an Alpine resort, so happily the restaurants offer far more than the usual ski staples of fondue and tartiflette. Fine French cooking goes hand in hand with global cuisine.

Try Japanese food at the ever popular **Satsuki** (p.80) or Asian fusion at uber-cool **Munchie** (p.79). Chamonix boasts a number of celebrity chefs; **Le Bistrot** in the base of hotel **Le Morgane** (p.23) is home to chef Mickey Bourdillat who was awarded a Michelin star for his simple cooking and dedication to pure flavours.

Beware the colourful restaurants in Chamonix town centre as they're often light on quality and heavy on expense. The best are worth scouting out and, if you feel like a bit of an adventure, some mountain restaurants are also open in the evening; try **Crèmerie du Glacier** (p.93) or **Les Vieilles Luges** (p.94).

Don't forget the numerous boulangeries dotted around town offering sandwiches, pizza slices and quiches as well as delicious bread. They are a handy value option if you are looking for a quick, cheap snack (p.70).

Vegetarian options

In a valley which specialises in making every conceivable combination of cheese and bread, vegetarians will have options in most places, even if variety is lacking. Savoyard salads are very popular and easy to find, as are omelettes and savoury crêpes. Both **Munchie** (p.79) and **Casa Valerio** (p.75) have good veggie choices and fish-eaters will enjoy **Satsuki** (p.80) and the upmarket **Atmosphere** (p.74).

Budget meals and take-aways

There is plenty of fast food on offer in Chamonix; **Mojo's** (p.79) in the centre of town offers healthy and delicious salads, sandwiches and wraps, whilst not for away is the calorific **Midnight Express** (p.78). Out at the western end of town **Belouga** (p.74) also provides fast, tasty snacks at reasonable prices. If it's pizza you're after, try

maddogski.com

Pizza Hop (p.80) or the speedy **Pizza Salsa** (p.80).

It would be nice to say that since the euro exchange rate took a hit, restaurants have lowered their prices. Unfortunately that's not the case. Make your pound go further by eating from the set menus offered by almost every restaurant and, of course, by picnicking on the mountain for lunch – our favourite bakeries and delis to stock up at are listed below. The good news is that in July 2009 VAT on food in France was reduced, which means that most restaurants have cut prices by 10%.

Local specialities

Tartiflette	popular enough to earn its own bumper stickers and Facebook groups, the trusted tartiflette is a hot, delicious concoction of reblochon, potatoes, cream and bacon
Fondue	a large vat of melted cheese (normally a combination of comté, beaufort and emmental) and wine is brought bubbling to your table for you to dip bread into. Usually ordered for two or more people
Pierrade	a rectangular piece of granite, heated by an electric element and coated with salt, on which chicken, beef and duck is self-cooked at the table
Raclette	a large half-moon of raclette cheese is placed under a heating element to melt. The gooey runoff is collected and eaten with pickles, potatoes and salad
Croûte au fromage	cheese, bread, fruit brandy and a little garlic; a hearty Alpine cheese on toast

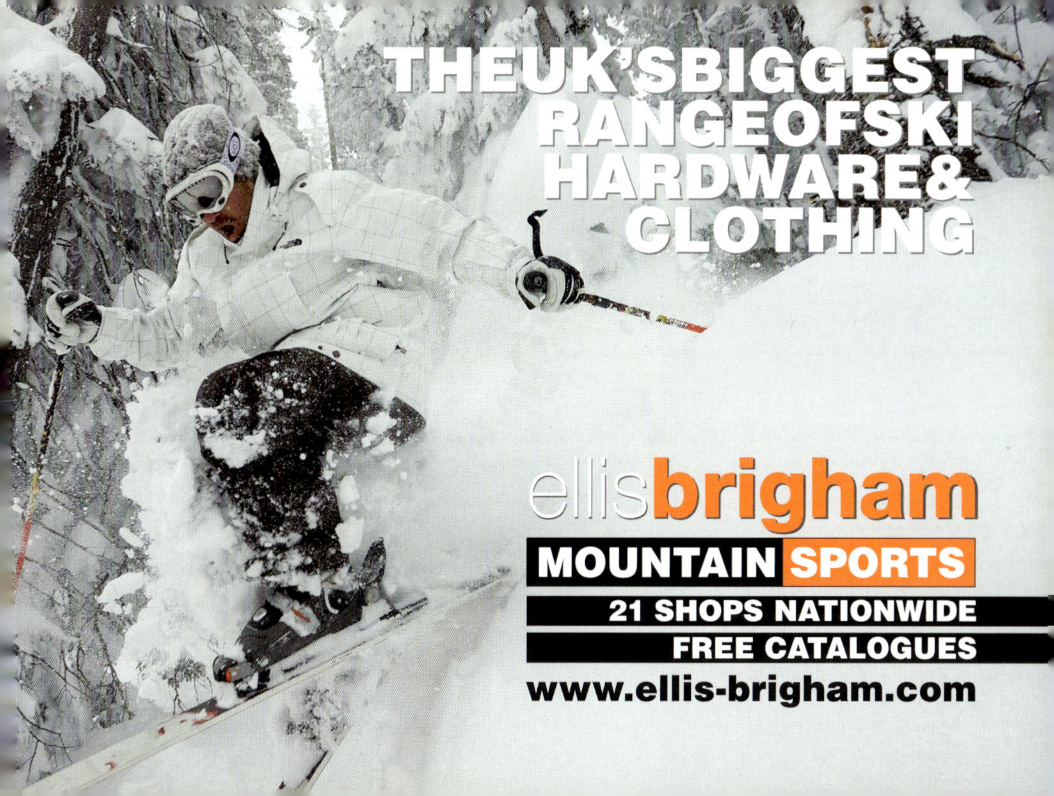

Bakeries

Chamonix, like much of France, has a near religious devotion to bakeries and warm croissants. It's not uncommon to find people boulangerie-hopping; getting bread at one place, croissants another and croque-monsieurs at yet another. This is our guide to helping you make the most of this great tradition.

Chamonix
Au Pain d'Antan (Ribeirou)
t +33 (0)4 50 53 40 88
118 Rue Whymper (just off Place du Mont Blanc).
Ribeirou sits opposite the Place du Mont Blanc, a short stroll from Chamonix centre. Pastries are on offer alongside slices of pizzas and sandwiches however most people come for the selection of breads. The delicious black olive bread and the chorizo bread are both great for picnics.

Chez Richard

t +33 (0)4 50 53 56 88
10 Rue du Docteur Paccard (opposite the Post Office).
This is our favourite and probably the best boulangerie in the valley. On the north-western edge of the main town square, Chez Richard is great for pretty much everything. All of the croissants here are perfect, in particular the chocolate and almond ones (€1.20) and the 'chausson pomme' (€1.30), which is a bit like an apple turnover.

Fleury Jean
t +33 (0)4 50 53 21 36
424 Rue Joseph Vallot.
Tucked away on the edge of town beyond Satsuki Japanese restaurant, on the road to Les Praz, Fleury Jean is a little gem. The croissants and bread are good, but what people really come for are the huge cookies; they are so good that they often sell out by 11am. Our absolute favourite is white chocolate and raspberry.

Le Fournil Chamoniard
t +33 (0)4 50 53 98 16
204 Avenue Aiguille du Midi (just a minute up the road from the Aiguille du Midi cable car).
Those heading off to tackle the Vallée Blanche can stock up here with croissants, sandwiches and the usual array of baguettes. The 'Brioche Suisse' (€1.50) with chocolate chips and éclair icing provides a compact sugar hit before you head up the hill.

Saint Hubert
t +33 (0)4 50 53 38 52
31 Place de l'Eglise (opposite the tourist office).
Just off the main square, St Hubert has lots of delicious fresh sandwiches from roast beef to cheese and ham to tuna mayo. Stop off on the way to Brévent or the bus stop.

Les Houches

Jacquier Eric
t +33 (0)4 50 54 40 76
106 Rue Mont Blanc, Les Houches (down the steps opposite the town hall).
A delightful bakery in the centre of Les Houches. You'll find quiches, pastries and baguettes in abundance, plus home made chocolates. Don't miss the 'Houchard', a concoction of custard, chocolate and pastry. If it's closed, they run a satellite branch opposite the Bellevue cable car which is open non-stop in high season.

maddogski.com

Chamonix town centre – restaurants

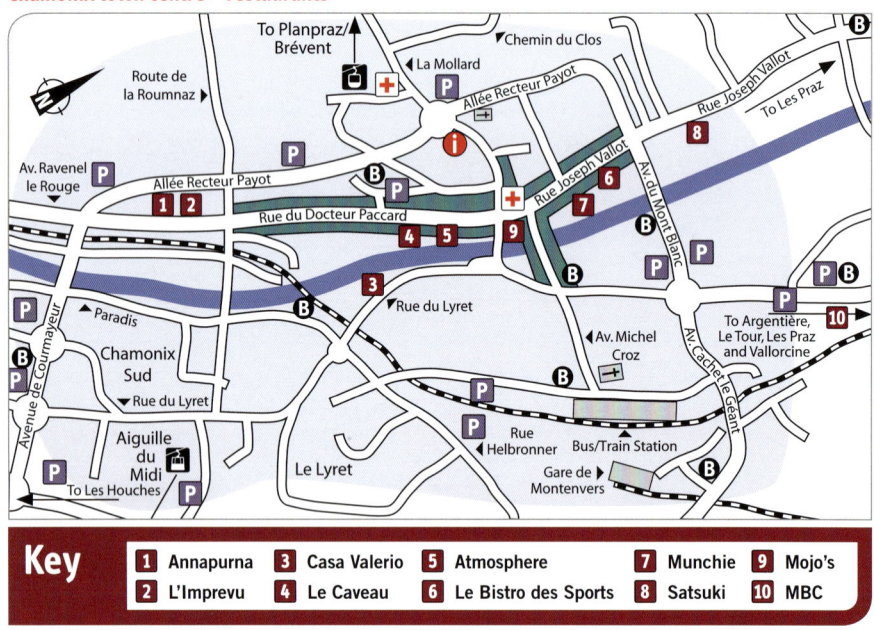

Key									
1	Annapurna	3	Casa Valerio	5	Atmosphere	7	Munchie	9	Mojo's
2	L'Imprevu	4	Le Caveau	6	Le Bistro des Sports	8	Satsuki	10	MBC

How to read our food and drink reviews

Budget: most main course prices are under €10/small beer costs around €3

Mid-range: main course prices range from €11-20/small beer costs €3-5

Expensive: most main course prices are €20+/small beer costs over €5

Our absolute Mad Dog favourites

Good vegetarian choice

Venues that stay open after 1am

Particularly good choice for children

Resort restaurants (p.74) and bars and clubs (p.82) are listed alphabetically by village. Mountain restaurants are listed by ski area (p.89).

maddogski.com

Resort restaurants
Chamonix
Annapurna
t +33 (0)4 50 55 81 39

62 Avenue Ravanel Le Rouge, on main pedestrian street towards the Vagabond hostel, 11am-3pm, 6pm-midnight.

An authentic Indian meal in the Alps. Tucked in at the western end of the high street, this family-run restaurant is intimate and cosy and the Indian dishes considered the best in the valley. Though there are some pricey things on the menu, the staples of chicken korma (€12) and rogan josh (€10) are very affordable. This is definitely the best place in Chamonix to get your curry fix.

Atmosphere
t +33 (0)4 50 55 97 97
w restaurant-atmosphere.com

123 Place Balmat, next to the Post Office, 6.30pm-midnight.

This elegant riverside restaurant has prime position on the main square. One of the resort's top restaurants, it's expensive, though well worth the money if you want a smart night out with plenty of pomp, including vacuum-toting waiters and immaculate white tablecloths. There is a good choice of set menus (€23-30 for three courses) which change every Thursday; check the board outside for options. Beware if you order the house special, lobster roasted with tomato and basil (€12 per 100g) – the waiter will bring him to your table for introductions before cooking… Reservations recommended.

Belouga
t +33 (0)4 50 18 47 26

56 Avenue Ravanel le Rouge, on main pedestrian street towards the Vagabond hostel, 11am-2am.

Belouga, a take-away counter, specialises in hot sandwiches and burgers and is open into the small hours. If in doubt, try the 'sunlight' burger with chive ('ciboulette') dressing (€4.70), or if you're in a rush just grab a generous tray of chips (€1.90).

Le Bistro des Sports
t +33 (0)4 50 53 00 46
w bistrotdessports.com

182 Rue Joseph Vallot, opposite Super U, 7am (Sunday 8am) until midnight.
This restaurant was founded in 1924 for the Olympic Games and has been a popular haunt ever since. The cuisine on offer is very traditional; try the classic 'Fondue Savoyarde' (€14.50 per person).

Casa Valerio
t +33 (0)4 50 55 93 40
w casavalerio.net

88 Rue Lyret, behind the Post Office, 12-2.30pm, 6.30-11.30pm.
Casa Valerio is the best loved and most popular Italian restaurant in the valley, and rightfully so. It's a warm, family-run place, where children are welcome and enthusiastic dining is encouraged. Pizza lovers will enjoy the calzone (€13), which is a folded pizza filled with ham, mushrooms, cheese and tomatoes. If you're more into your pasta go for the unforgettable Spaghetti al gamberoni (€16) with a brace of langoustines on top. Reservations recommended.

Our absolute favourite restaurants... and why

Atmosphere (p.74)	modern French restaurant with riverside setting
Casa Valerio (p.75)	jolly Italian restaurant with something for everyone
Mojo's (p.79)	fresh sandwiches on-the-run
Munchie (p.79)	Asian fusion in a modern setting. Fantastic duck teriyaki

maddogski.com

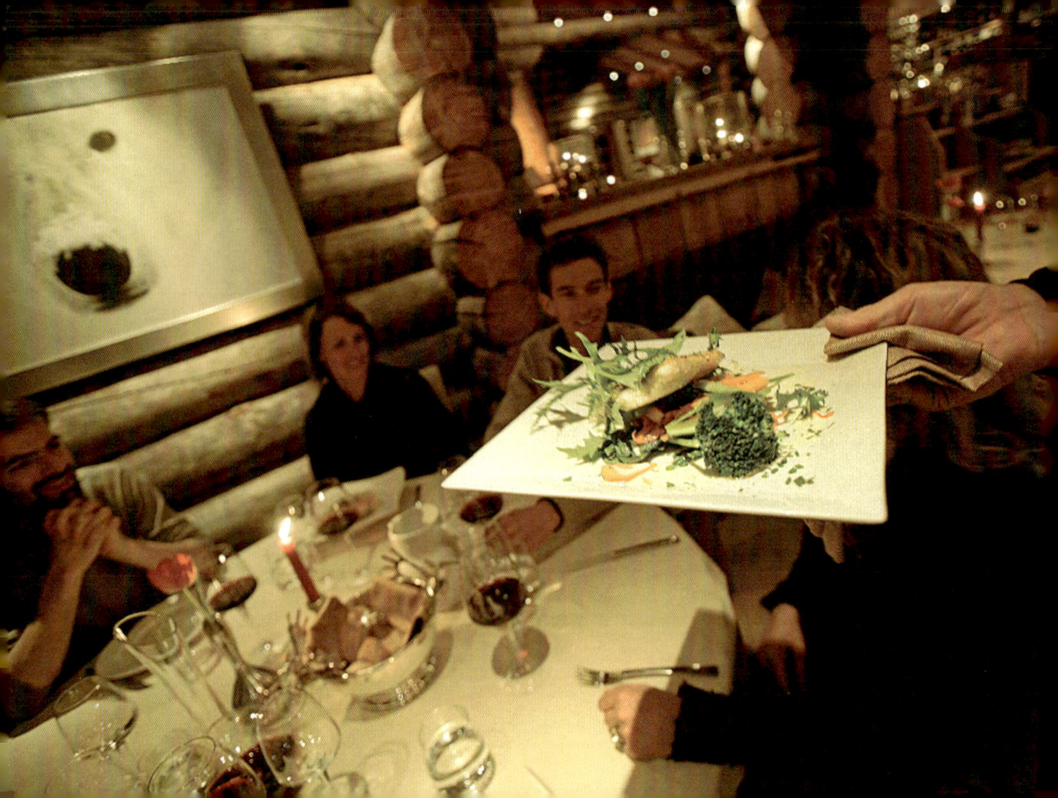

Le Caveau
t +33 (0)4 50 55 86 18

🪙 LATE

13 Rue du Docteur Paccard, next to the Post Office (entrance is tucked in next to Chez Yang), 6.30pm-2am.

A relaxed restaurant offering dishes from around the globe including rich Swedish meatballs (€14), stone baked pizzas and great garlic bread filled with mozzarella. One of the attractions of the restaurant is its unique underground location in the centre of town. The arched stone caves date back more than 300 years and have in their time served as sheep pen, wine cellar, nightclub and now restaurant.

Elevation 1904
t +33 (0)4 50 53 00 52

🪙

259 Avenue Michel Croz, opposite the train station, 7.30am-about 10pm.

Elevation is a hive of activity year round and an ideal choice for those wanting a quick and easy bite to eat. Breakfast, lunch or supper, eat in or take-away, Elevation has it covered. Small, inexpensive and relaxed, offering everything from salads to panini, steaks and pasta. The pineappley Hawaiian burgers (€5.90) or house salads (€9.50) are both easy lunches. The English breakfast makes a change from the usual croissant, butter and jam offered elsewhere.

L'impossible
t +33 (0)4 50 53 20 36
w restaurant-impossible.com

🪙

9 Chemin du Cry, just before the hospital, 7pm-1am.

Set in an old Savoyard farmhouse a few minutes from the edge of the town, L'impossible embraces local style with its fascinating interior and, more importantly, its food. The chefs take tradition and good quality ingredients seriously and produce wonderful regional dishes. Try the onion gratin soup (€7.50) or three-course set menu (€22.50). The warm, welcoming ambience and delicious food are hard to fault. Reservations are always recommended.

L'Imprevu
t +33 (0)4 50 53 96 74

24 Avenue Ravanel le Rouge, on main pedestrian street towards the Vagabond hostel, 12-2.30pm, 6.30-10pm.

A favourite with the locals, L'Imprevu is a hotspot for good home cooking at reasonable prices. The set menus, from €16.90, are a wise choice for snails, fondue and pudding. For the carnivores, the steaks here are mouth-watering too. Unusually, they serve single order fondues.

Micro Brasserie de Chamonix
t +33 (0)4 50 53 61 59
w mbchx.com

350 Route Bouchet, opposite the sports centre, food from 4-11pm, drinks served until midnight.

Known locally as the 'MBC', the Micro Brasserie de Chamonix is one of the most popular après-ski establishments in Chamonix (p.86) and makes a lively dinner venue. Particularly busy on Mondays, when punters are able to enjoy half price chicken wings. Reservations are recommended.

Midnight Express
LATE

9 Rue du Docteur Paccard, in the main square, next to the Post Office, 10.30am-2am.

Most Chamoniards pass through Midnight Express at some time or other. Set right in the centre of town, Midnight is usually the first port of call after the bars close and party animals are booted out. Perfect for a tasty, if calorific, bite to eat. The 'Orient' baguette (€3.70) is very good; don't be surprised to see chips inside the baguette – that's normal here.

Mad Dog Ski Chamonix

Mojo's

t +33 (0)4 50 89 12 26

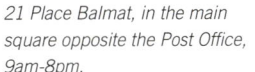

21 Place Balmat, in the main square opposite the Post Office, 9am-8pm.

Bang in the centre of town, Mojo's serves delicious, fresh, hot and cold sandwiches. Enjoy their legendary sushi wrap or chicken-and-bacon Mojo One (both €5.50). Sure you pay a bit more, but the food is less sinful than other fast-food places and is freshly made in front of you. There's a highly sociable, highly sunny terrace outside and a couple of internet-connected computers inside.

Munchie

t +33 (0)4 50 53 45 41
w munchie.eu

79 Rue du Moulins, between Super U and the river, 7pm-1am.

At the top of every Chamoniard's list of places to eat is the renowned Munchie. The Asian fusion dishes are a bit pricey, but worth it – perhaps best of all are the duck teriyaki (€21) and the Korean spicy seafood hotpot (€21). Munchie's reputation has spread far and wide and the restaurant pulls in hungry diners from Geneva and other distant areas, not to mention locals and tourists. For this reason, booking in advance is essential.

Pizza Hop
t +33 (0)4 50 53 90 40

269 Avenue Courmayeur, opposite Les Aiglons hotel, 5-11pm.
Pretty much the Domino's of the Chamonix Valley (though sadly they don't deliver), Pizza Hop produce quality, decent value pizza. They take around 15 minutes so it's a good idea to ring ahead with your order. If in doubt, our favourite is a La Reine pizza with ham and mushrooms (€8).

Pizza Salsa
t +33 (0)4 50 53 96 90

215 Avenue Michel Croz, near the train station, 11am-10pm.
The perfect pit stop for pizza on-the-run. They take around 10 minutes to make you a delicious pizza. There are a couple of picnic tables on their terrace, and they do take-away too. We always get the Antillaise (€7.70), their oregano-rich take on a Hawaiian.

Poco Loco
t +33 (0)4 50 53 43 03

47 Rue du Docteur Paccard, on main street between the Post Office and Snell Sports, 11am-midnight for take-away, midday-midnight inside.
Tasty burgers (from €5) and chunky chips are the best reason to visit Poco Loco. Conveniently situated in the centre of town and equipped with a small but significant indoor seating area; you can also sneak upstairs for a private feast.

Satsuki
t +33 (0)4 50 53 21 99
w satsuki.eu

288 Rue Joseph Vallot, before Hotel Boule de Neige on the Les Praz road, 12-2pm, 6.30-10pm.
Satsuki is a wonderful little Japanese restaurant a few minutes' walk from the centre of town, close to the Alpina Hotel. The Japanese staff are multilingual and helpful and the food authentic and delicious. If you are looking for value, grab an off-slope set menu

lunch (€8.80); try the teriyaki chicken, which comes with miso soup and green tea. And of course the sushi (€20 for a plate for two) is fantastic. Reservations are essential during peak season.

Argentière restaurants
Taxis from Chamonix to Argentière take 15 minutes (expect to pay around €35).

Le Dahu
t +33 (0)4 50 54 01 55
w hotel-le-dahu.com

Hôtel Le Dahu, 325 Rue Charlet Straton, Argentière (on main street), 12-2pm, 7-10pm.
It's rare to find a good and reasonably priced French restaurant like Le Dahu amongst the bright lights of a ski village. Understated, delicious local dishes like trout meunière (€13.50) or onion soup (€7) are brought to you by friendly and efficient staff. The quick-fire, good quality lunch menu (€13) is particularly recommended.

The Rusticana
t +33 (0)4 50 55 88 28
w therusty.net

216 Rue Charlet Straton, Argentière (on main street), 3pm-1am.
Known affectionately as 'The Rusty' and beloved of the ex-pat community, you can enjoy food from around the world and (most importantly to the Brits) the best fish and chips in the area (€12). The Rusty is also popular as a bar, because of the finger-licking snacks on offer, from chicken spring rolls with chilli dip (€6) to ham, egg and chip platters (€9).

Les Praz restaurants
In the evening, you can get to nearby Les Praz by foot (15 minutes), a short taxi journey (around €20) or, if eating at the Hotel Eden, you can use their free pickup service.

If you are in the village for the evening, a good place for a few apres-ski drinks is the **Rhodos** bar (p.89), which you'll find in the middle of the green.

maddogski.com

La Cabane
t +33 (0)4 50 53 23 27
w restaurant-lacabane.com

La Cabane des Praz, at the golf course, 12-2.30pm, 7-11pm.
The short walk out of the town centre to the beautiful hamlet of Les Praz is well worth it for a visit to La Cabane. Set in a classic wooden lodge just a few hundred metres from the base of the Flégère cable car, the restaurant specialises in contemporary French cuisine. Brave souls will relish the snails in garlic butter however be assured that there is plenty to tempt those with a less adventurous palate, such as the tender beef fillet (€28).

Restaurant Eden
t +33 (0)4 50 53 18 43
w hoteleden-chamonix.com

35 Route des Gaudenays, Les Praz, behind the church next to the level crossing, 6-10pm (closed Tuesday evenings).
Near the bottom of the Flégère lift, both the restaurant and Hotel Eden have won rave reviews from guides, including the Michelin. The relaxed atmosphere and service combined with delicious contemporary cuisine ensure that diners feel welcome while munching treats like tempura sea bass (€16) or one of the set menus (€19 or €26). Don't let the roadside location fool you; this place is really special. Call for details of free pickup service. Reservations recommended.

Après-ski and nightlife
Despite its reputation as a serious, get-up-early-and-get-mountaineering resort, Chamonix knows how to have a good time. Since the home runs are rarely in skiable shape, everyone is forced to take cable cars and gondolas down to town, when they generally make a rush to the hot après places. Hence the action centres around a couple of specific bars which are popular every evening, especially from 4-7pm. And like many resorts, it's not uncommon to find that you're still wearing ski boots at 1am.

Most bars sell Amstel as their draught beer of choice, but you'll also find Heineken, Stella, Magners and even Guiness on tap. Shot culture prevails, with lots of bars offering their own goosebumpy alternative to the ubiquitous Jägerbomb, a shot of dark liqueur dropped into a tumbler of Red Bull.

Opening times aren't specified as they vary throughout the season. Generally bars open around 3pm and close by 1am. After that, there are a few late night options – try **Le Garage** (p.85) or **La Terrace** (p.87).

Chamonix
Bar'd Up
t +33 (0)4 50 53 91 33

123 rue des Moulins, opposite the Hotel Alpina, next to the river.

If there was spit and sawdust in the Alps, it would all blow into Bar d'Up. The seediness of the place comprises most of its appeal (although a visit to the toilets may have you thinking otherwise). Bar'd Up is so ski town they have a draught Jagermeister machine. The low ceilings, fish tanks and big-screen TVs build atmosphere, the pool table is busy, the table football constantly in use and the

Our absolute favourite bars... and why

Chambre Neuf (p.85)	live music and plenty of beer makes for loud après-ski
Le Lapin Agile (p.85)	a chilled, tiny wine bar
MBC (p.86)	a Chamonix institution; microbrewery and live music
Les Rhodos (p.89)	a warm welcome and great value. Worth the walk!

maddogski.com

Chamonix town centre – bars and clubs

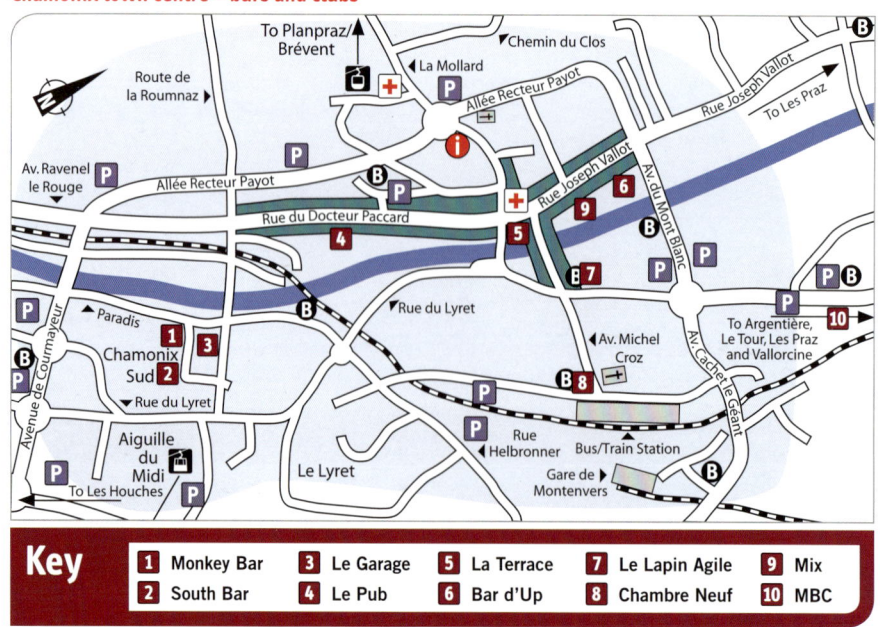

Key

1 Monkey Bar	3 Le Garage	5 La Terrace	7 Le Lapin Agile	9 Mix
2 South Bar	4 Le Pub	6 Bar d'Up	8 Chambre Neuf	10 MBC

Mad Dog Ski Chamonix

darts always flying. No doubt you'll know from that description whether to visit or stay away.

Chambre Neuf
t +33 (0)4 50 53 00 31

272 Avenue Michel-Croz, opposite the train station.
Something of a classic resort bar, Chambre has excellent live music every afternoon and is the default spot for an after-snow beer. The Swedish-run place gets packed, partly due to the 'anything goes' attitude of the blonde-haired, blue-eyed bar staff.

People who live and work in the resort often prefer to turn up later in the evening, once the band has packed up and gone home, the atmosphere is calmer and there's more chance of bagging themselves a table.

Le Garage
t +33 (0)6 33 76 86 00
w nightclublegarage.com

213 Avenue de l'Aiguille du Midi, opposite the Hotel Morgane.
As one of Chamonix's few late-night places, Le Garage enjoys a virtual monopoly over the town's midnight-oil-burners. Drinks are abusively expensive (around €7 for a beer) but are bought in abundance in the swarthy, darkened surroundings. Music is almost exclusively Euro-pop, and the dancefloor always packed. Curiously, it bears an inexplicable magnetism over the town and is full most nights.

Le Lapin Agile
t +33 (0)4 50 53 33 25
w lelapinagile.fr

11 Rue Whymper, opposite McDonald's.
The Lapin is a tiny place with only five or six tables. It's an Italian wine bar to which you'd be happy to bring your parents, and as such is sidestepped by most of the holidaymakers in town. That only contributes to the in-the-know vibe. Free tapas from 6.30-9pm.

maddogski.com

Micro Brasserie de Chamonix
t +33 (0)4 50 53 61 59
w mbchx.com

350 Route de Bouchet, opposite the sports centre, 4pm-midnight.
The location may be a little out of the centre but the fact remains; MBC rocks. The Canadian-owned microbrewery makes their own beer on site, and a sip of their Granite Pale Ale will undoubtedly assure you that quality most certainly leads to quantity, especially when washed down with their crunchy nachos (€8.75 for two people) and sticky chicken wings (€10.50 for 12, half-price on Monday nights). The joke goes that most of the British Mountaineering Club can be found in the Micro Brewery Chamonix, and it's not far from the truth.

Mix
t +33 (0)6 11 14 96 71

90 Rue des Moulins, opposite Munchie.
Had Mix been in any other town in the world, it could be described as snooty. However, since bars like this are so lacking around Chamonix, Mix has carved quite a niche for itself. Airy and modern, with lots of steel and stone, the drinks are expensive but feel worth it; fancy glasses, premium beers and frequent bar snacks. Useful for dates or special occasions.

Monkey Bar
t +33 (0)4 50 96 64 34

81 Place Edmond Desailloud, Chamonix Sud.
This bar is a favourite amongst Brits thanks to its Cham Sud location – the seedier end of town, right in amongst the low-cost seasonnaire accommodation. Their Sunday night roast dinners are amazing, however this isn't really a restaurant; get a round of pool in, gawp at the photo-realistic murals, and tuck in. A really authentic ski-town haunt.

Mad Dog Ski Chamonix

Munster
t +33 (0)4 50 18 46 38
w munsterbar.com

27 Place Edmond Desailloud, Chamonix Sud (opposite the Monkey Bar).
This busy Irish-owned bar is a firm favourite with the Brits in town. There are often big-screen sports showing on enormous plasma screens above the bar. Their tremendous fancy-dress 80s-themed parties are always very popular amongst the sizeable ex-pat community.

Le Pub
t +33 (0)4 50 55 92 88

225 Rue du Docteur Paccard, on the main street.
This establishment merits a mention thanks to its warm welcome, central location, high ceilings, extensive selection of beer and heated outdoor seating. It's aimed at the Brit crowd and is popular, especially on sports nights when the big screens are always out.

South Bar
t +33 (0)4 50 53 98 56
w southbar.se

83 Place Edmond Desalloud, Chamonix Sud.
Whilst every other tourist in town flocks to Chambre Neuf for a taste of Swedish après-ski Chamonix style, saunter down to South Bar and hang out with Scandinavian pro skiers, Finnish film crews and Chambre staff on their night off. South Bar often has live music, but more importantly always has good cold beer and a warm welcome.

La Terrace
t +33 (0)4 50 53 09 95
w laterrassechamonix.com

43 Place Balmat, opposite the Casino.

Food and drink Après-ski

maddogski.com

The gaudy, purple-hued exterior of this riverside bar belies a roomy, airy interior. Locals head upstairs to the first-floor bar to enjoy the balcony tables and roomier surroundings. If you can't miss that all-important football game or Formula One race, you'll generally find it on at La Terrace.

Argentière
Slalom Bar

Rue Charlet Stratton, opposite the Dahu.
This tiny bar is the must-stop-by location for the Argentière après-skier. There's a bookshelf with plenty of English titles and free tapas served from 6-8pm. Sit

on the tiny terrace and watch the world go by.

Les Praz
Les Rhodos
t +33 (0)4 50 53 06 39
w lesrhododendrons.com

100 Route des Tines, Les Praz (on the village green).

This sprawling hotel bar is right next to the church on the middle of the green in Les Praz. As the nearest bar to the La Flégère bottom station, it's busy at après time and worth stopping by. The restaurant frequently runs 'beer & pizza' promotions.

Mountain Restaurants

This section reviews your options for eating on the mountain. **We've given details of the restaurants, along with full reviews of our favourite places. Every review has a number in red beside it. You can check the location on the piste map (p.90).**

Sadly, Chamonix's gastronomy at altitude leaves a lot to be desired; the majority of the restaurants are head-in-trough, American-style canteen affairs with shocking prices (€10 for onion soup, and worse) and little atmosphere. Many choose to have a huge breakfast, ski all day and live it up over dinner in one of the town's excellent restaurants.

Brévent – Flégère
Bergerie ❶
t +33(0)4 50 53 05 42

Lifts/Pedestrian: Planpraz gondola.
Although most visitors head straight for the Panoramique restaurant at the 2325m top station, those in the know stop by the Bergerie at Planpraz. There's more room, less of a price hike and better quality meals. Although the food is self-service canteen-style downstairs, it's pretty good for the money. You'll find more expensive à la carte table-service dining upstairs, with two sittings (midday and 1.45pm).

maddogski.com

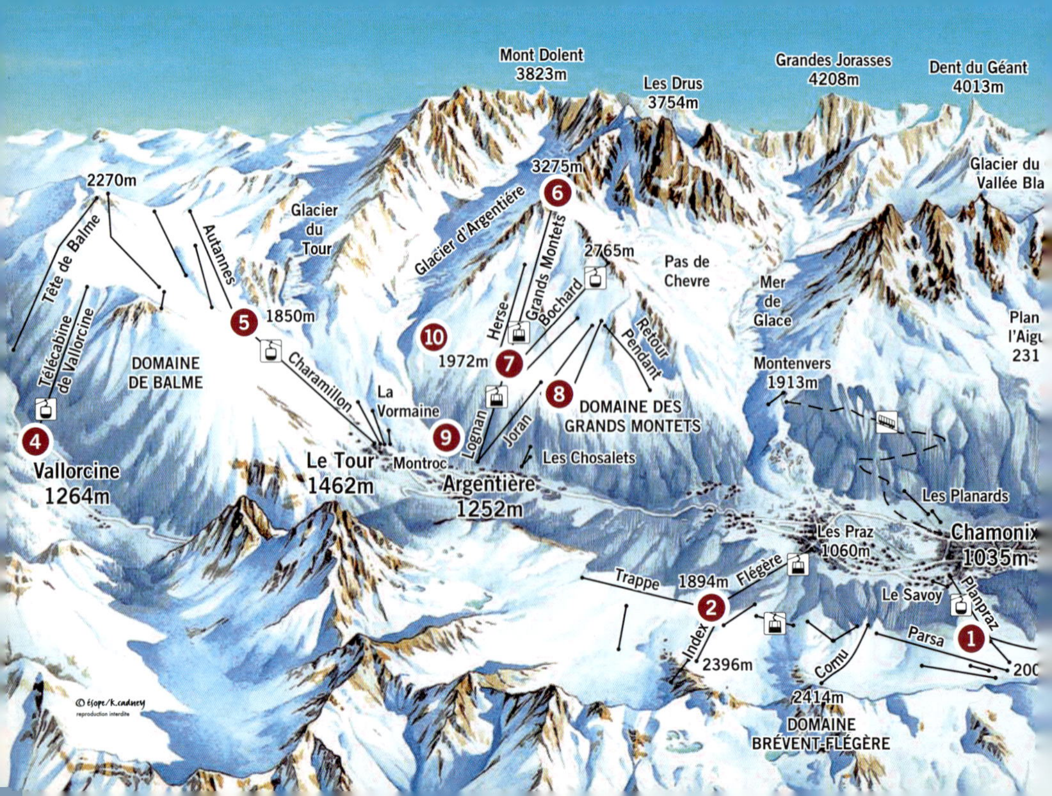
Mont Dolent
3823m
Les Drus
3754m
Grandes Jorasses
4208m
Dent du Géant
4013m
2270m
3275m
6
Glacier du
Vallée Bla
Glacier
du
Tour
Glacier d'Argentiére
Grands Montets
2765m
Pas de
Chevre
Tête de Balme
Autannes
Bochard
Mer
de
Glace
Herse
Retour
Pendant
Plan
l'Aigu
231
5
1850m
10
Télécabine
de Vallorcine
Charamillon
DOMAINE
DE BALME
1972m
7
Montenvers
1913m
La
Vormaine
8
DOMAINE DES
GRANDS MONTETS
4
9
Lognan
Joran
Les Chosalets
Vallorcine
1264m
Le Tour
1462m
Montroc
Argentière
1252m
Les Planards
Les Praz
1060m
Chamonix
1035m
Trappe
1894m
Flégère
2
Le Savoy
Planpraz
Index
Parsa
1
2396m
Comu
200
2414m
DOMAINE
BRÉVENT-FLÉGÈRE
© ésope/k.cadney
reproduction interdite

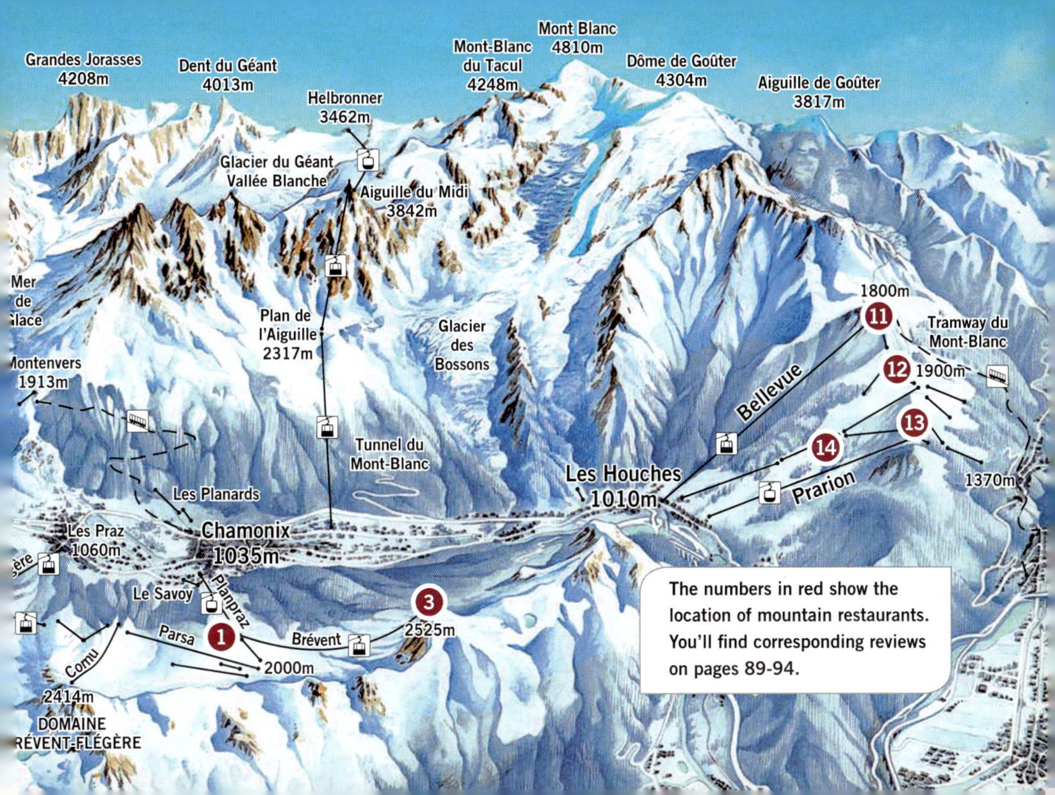

The numbers in red show the location of mountain restaurants. You'll find corresponding reviews on pages 89-94.

La Flégère Cafeteria ②
t +33(0)4 50 55 34 88

Lifts/Pedestrian: at the top of the Flégère cable car and at the base of **Pylones** *and* **Piste de Liason**.

Le Panoramique ③
t +33 (0)4 50 53 44 11

Lifts/Pedestrian: at the top of the Brévent cable car, and the top of the **Charles Bozon** *run.*
This restaurant is accessible to skiers of all levels – if you don't fancy skiing, you can take the cable car down.

Le Tour
L'Arrete Bougnete ④
t +33 (0) 4 50 54 63 04

Lifts/Pedestrian: at the bottom of **Forêt Verte**, *just as you're walking back towards the gondola, you'll see this little place bolted onto the side of Vallorcine station.*
The service here is spectacular and the terrace is always in glorious sunlight. Inside, the walls are covered with mountain bric-a-brac; old snowshoes and cross-country skis. The place has a real chalet atmosphere and there are often pro skiers nipping in to order sandwiches (ham, cheese and pickle, €4.50) that they'll pick up the following run.

Chalet de Charamillon ⑤
t +33(0)4 50 54 04 72

Lifts/Pedestrian: at the top of the Le Tour Charamillon gondola and the base of **Retour Charamillon**.

Les Grands Montets
Aiguille des Grands Montets ⑥

Lifts/Pedestrian: Grands Montets cable car top station.
You tend to lose your appetite over two miles (3275m) above sea level, so thankfully the food options are light (bowls of soup, various sandwiches, omelettes) at this tiny little café perched at the top of the Les Grands Montets area. The views out of the slit-like windows

Mad Dog Ski Chamonix

are breathtaking and it's the perfect place to grab a quick skier's lunch while adapting to the altitude.

Cafeteriere du Lognan 7
t +33 (0)4 50 54 10 21

Lifts/Pedestrian: in the Lognan mid-station at the bottom of Marmottons and Bochard.

Cafeteria Plan Joran 8
t +33 (0)4 50 54 05 77

Lifts: 200m from the top of the Plan Joran chairlift and the bottom of Marmottons and Coqs.
Pedestrian: no access.

Crèmerie du Glacier 9
t +33 (0)4 50 54 07 52

Lifts: Lognan cable car.
Pedestrian: a 10 minute walk; next to Pierre à Ric from the Grands Montets car park or by car (limited parking outside).

Although its pine interior makes it feel something like a sauna, the Crèmerie dates back to 1926 and is one of the oldest mountain restaurants in the valley. The original owner built the place using money earned from selling ice from the Argentière glacier. The suppers are good, but there's nothing like pulling up outside on your skis to enjoy a mushroom fondue for lunch. The omelettes are also classic French and delicious. Reservations recommended.

Refuge Lognan 10
t +33(0)6 88 56 03 54

Lifts: Herse chairlift or Grands Montets cable car.
Pedestrian: no access.

The Lognan refuge has a 25 bed dormitory upstairs if you fancy spending an evening in the mountains, however most of us head there on our way back from the **Point de Vue** piste, when we can't bear to leave behind the view over the glacier. The food is traditional and the service particularly good.

maddogski.com

Les Houches
Chalette ⑪
t +33 (0)4 50 54 41 99

Lifts/Pedestrian: at the exit of the Bellevue cable car.

Courant d'air ⑫
t +33 (0)4 50 54 40 04

Lifts: Bellevue or Prarion gondolas; restaurant is at the Col de Voza, halfway between the two top stations. Pedestrian: no access.

Hotel le Prarion ⑬
t +33 (0)4 50 54 40 07

Lifts/Pedestrian: Prarion gondola top station.

Les Vieilles Luges ⑭
t +33 (0)6 84 42 37 00
w lesvieillesluges.com

Lifts: Maison Neuve chairlift, Prarion gondola. Pedestrian: evenings only (see below).
This charming, rickety restaurant is nestled in the forest just off the Aillouds run at Les Houches; a short but windy traverse opens up a clearing under the Maison Neuve chairlift where the restaurant is perched. The valley's best vin chaud is served here. Suppers are particularly special; with the lift closed, you'll have to crampon, skin or snowshoe for half an hour to get to the restaurant. It's well worth it and fondue doesn't seem quite so extravagant after the exercise. Reservations essential for both lunch and supper.

Can't ski, won't ski? Too much snow or not enough? Find out about the many **other things to do** in Chamonix.

What you'll find in this chapter

Non-skiing activities..................97
Shopping..............................101

Non-skiing activities

Chamonix is a hive of activity throughout the winter season so there's plenty to keep non-skiers entertained. The Chamonix valley is famous for its spectacular scenery and there are several sightseeing tours which allow you to get close to it. The trip up the cable car to the Aiguille du Midi is a must-do, as is the excursion to the Mer du Glace glacier and ice cave. Of course, aside from the mountain adventures, the more standard winter activities like snow shoeing, dog sledding and paragliding are all popular too. Activities that are particularly suitable for younger children are marked with our kid-friendly symbol. They can be useful time fillers once ski school is finished.

Bowling
Bowling de Chamonix
t +33 (0)4 50 53 74 37
w bowling-chamonix.com

196 Avenue Courmayeur.
For bad weather days and evenings, Chamonix's 10-pin bowling alley provides everything you need. Upstairs you'll find snooker and pool tables - and a mini golf course!

Casino
Casino de Barriere du Chamonix
w lucienbarriere.com
12 Place Saussure (opposite the Post Office).
This grandiose building dominates the centre of town, looking as if it would be more at home in Monte Carlo than Mont Blanc. The casino remains the place to dispose of those unwanted euro cluttering up your pockets. Smart dress a must.

Cinema
Le Vox
t + 33 (0)4 50 53 03 39
w cinemavox-chamonix.com

22 Cour du Bartavel (between the Post Office and tourist office).
Films in English are regularly shown at Le Vox, but usually run a few months behind UK box office releases. Programmes are available from reception or on the website. English films are suffixed 'VO' to indicate that they are

shown with English audio and French subtitles.

Climbing
Mont Blanc Escalade
t +33 (0)4 50 54 76 48
w montblancescalade.com
ZA des Trabets, Les Houches (down the hill from the Bellevue cable car base station), 12-10pm.
With the popular outdoor Gaillands climbing area out of action in the winter (too cold and icy), many head to the indoor wall in Les Houches. There are over 40 routes so you can find something to challenge every level of climber – up to a staggering 9a. Entry is a reasonable €12.50.

Dog sledding
Guide a team of dogs across the snow, through woods and open fields in spectacular surroundings. The experience begins with an introduction to your team followed by lessons in how to handle and control your canine chums. You then set out on a trek, with you at the wheel. Prices are from €40 per person including a lift to the departure point.

Evolution 2
t +33 (0)4 50 55 90 22
w evolution2-chamonix.com
350 Avenue de la Plage.

Huskydalen
t +33 (0)4 50 47 77 24
w huskydalen.com

Other things to do

Gym and swimming
Centre Sportif
t +33 (0)4 50 53 23 70

Centre Sportif Richard Bozon, 214 Avenue de la Plage, 12-8pm. Fitness junkies will find a gym and swimming pool at the sports centre. Gentlemen; if you fancy a swim bear in mind that in France, for some unknown 'hygiene purposes', tight 'Speedo' type trunks are mandatory!

Helicopter rides
Chamonix Mont-Blanc Helico
t +33 (0)4 50 54 13 82
w chamonix-helico.fr

For those not wanting to get up close and personal with a glacier or the mountains, you don't have to miss out on the experience. A helicopter ride offers an unforgettable – though pretty expensive – way to see the valley. Prices start at €65 for a 15 minute flight, leaving from the helipad at the base of the Argentière glacier.

Ice skating
Centre Sportif Richard Bozon
t +33 (0)4 50 53 23 70

214 Avenue de la Plage, 12-8pm. There's an ice rink at the town's sports centre and skaters of all ages are welcome – admission is around €5 and skate rental a couple of euro extra. The rink measures 30m x 60m and has an adjoining restaurant and bar which are good for a snack whilst watching local pros pirouetting and twirling around on the ice.

maddogski.com

Museums and art galleries
Alpine Museum
t +33 4 50 53 25 93
89 Avenue Michel Croz, every afternoon 2-7pm.
The Alpine Museum in the centre of town is home to an extensive collection of exhibits covering the ecology, history, flora and fauna of the region. Entry €5.

Gallery du Globe
t +33 4 50 54 54 54
w galerieduglobe.com
93 rue Charlet Straton, Argentière.
This gallery opened in 2007 and features eight artists including photographers, painters and ceramists. The café is open Tuesday to Friday from 3-7.30pm and Saturday and Sunday from 11am-7.30pm.

Paragliding
Les Ailes Du Mont Blanc
t +33 (0)4 50 53 96 72
w lesailesdumontblanc.com
24 Avenue de la Plage.

Summit Professional Training
t +33 (0)4 50 53 50 14
e summits@summits.fr
Le Mummery, 27 Allée du Savoy.
Take a running jump off the side of a mountain for what is one of the most exhilarating experiences on offer in the valley. Jumps are always tandem so there's really very little to do but gaze at the view and take photos. Expect to pay around €100 per jump.

Other things to do

Sightseeing: The Aiguille du Midi and the Mer de Glace
Compagnie du Mont Blanc
t +33 (0)4 50 53 22 75
w compagniedumontblanc.fr

At a dizzying 3842m above sea level, the view from the Aiguille is well worth the effort, the scary cable car ride and the €36 ticket.

If you prefer your mountain adventures closer to the ground, the Montenvers train is a good excursion. This is one of the oldest rack-and-pinion railways in France and it ferries tourists up from Chamonix to Europe's second longest glacier – the Mer de Glace.

Once off the train visitors can take a gondola, then a set of stairs, down to the glacier and check out the sculptures in the ice cave.

Snow shoeing
Compagnie des Guides
t + 33 (0)4 50 53 00 88
w chamonix-guides.com
Maison de la Montagne, 190 Place de l'Eglise.

Snow shoeing allows you to enjoy the beauty of the valley in peace and tranquillity. Tours are generally guided, not only so you can find the way but also so you can learn about the flora and fauna in the woods. Good exercise, good fun and hopefully you'll learn something too. From €40 per person for a two-hour trip (includes gear).

Swimming
See under **Gym**.

Shopping
Chamonix is a shopper's dream when it comes to high quality mountain gear, winter clothing, skis and snowboards. But that's not all – there's tons of great food and drink available as well as plenty of boutiques. Big brands love Chamonix and signature stores jostle for position all down the main pedestrian shopping street, Rue du Docteur Paccard. Amongst others you'll find Lacoste, Chanel, Esprit and Swarovski.

Shops generally start their day around 9am and close at 7pm. Most are closed between 1-2pm minimum; some lucky workers enjoy a three-hour lunch break. Hours can vary depending on weather and busy periods – if it's essential, phone ahead to check.

maddogski.com

Food and wine

Self-catering is very popular in Chamonix and most of the villages have at least one food shop.

Chamonix centre
Super U
Rue Joseph Vallot, open all day Monday to Saturday and on Sunday mornings.

Casino
These smaller grocery stores are dotted around Chamonix. Open until 8pm and on Sunday afternoons.

Les Houches
Super U (Le Borgeat)
Just outside St Antoine, open Monday to Saturday.

There are plenty of places to stock up on the main street in Argentière and Vallorcine and Les Praz has a small village shop (Route des Praz).

For bakeries and delis see p.70.

Cha Cha Cha
t +33 (0)4 50 93 47 74
w chachacha74.blogspot.com
134 Avenue Ravanel le Rouge.
Stop by Cha Cha Cha for a bottle and discover wines from all over the world. It's a classy wine merchant where you are welcome to stay and sample before buying. Wine tasting evenings take place several nights a week from 6-9pm and cost €15 per person – this price gives you at least six glasses of wine.

La Refuge Payot
t +33 (0)4 50 53 18 71
w refugepayot.com
166 Rue Joseph Vallot.
t +33 (0)4 50 53 16 86
255 Rue du Docteur Paccard.
La Refuge Payot stocks Savoyard specialities including cheese, meat, wine and liquors which are proudly sold in two large shops at either end of the town. These are handy places to pick up local food and gifts to take home.

If you are looking to try some local cheeses, popular choices are Reblochon (one of the essential ingredients for tartiflette) and creamy Beaufort. If in doubt, ask for some help choosing.

Other things to do

and greatest in every form of mountaineering gear you can possibly imagine. You could happily spend a couple of hours here indulging yourself in tech-head-heaven… and many people do.

Solaris
t +33 (0)4 50 55 95 75
17 Place Balmat (on the main square).
High quality protective eyewear.

Ski equipment and clothes
Helly Hansen
t +33 (0)4 50 53 65 61
w hellyhansen-chamonix.com
284 Rue du Docteur Paccard.
For high quality, classic mountain and ski wear.

Snell Sports
t +33 (0)4 50 53 02 17
w cham3s.com
104 Rue du Docteur Paccard.
This is as close as you get to a department store in Chamonix. The huge store stocks the latest

Zero G Chamonix
t +33 (0)4 50 53 01 01
w zerogchx.com
90 Ravanel le Rouge.
Tucked away at the end of the main street in Chamonix, Zero G is a gem best known for its hard

maddogski.com

goods and outerwear, but venture upstairs and you will find an Aladdin's cave of funky streetwear. Friendly and helpful staff.

Books and newsagents

There are plenty of tabacs around the town selling newspapers, sweets, postcards, stamps, phone top-ups and cigarettes.

Maison de la Presse

t +33 (0)4 50 53 29 76
93 Rue du Docteur Paccard.
Maison de la Presse stocks a large number of books and magazines in French and English. Downstairs you will find a stationery shop, and outside a huge quantity of postcards.

Mad Dog Ski Chamonix

Skiing with **children**... dream or nightmare? A little planning goes a long way.

What you'll find in this chapter
Accommodation 107
Childcare 112
Ski school 112
Restaurants 112

Chamonix is known for its challenging terrain and extensive off-piste more than for being an obvious choice for young families. If your children are new to skiing we wouldn't recommend it.

If your children are already competent skiers then there's plenty to enjoy if you're happy with the commuting to the slopes that's practically a given in Chamonix. In spite of the drawbacks, if you do find yourself here with kids to entertain, there's a reasonable amount on offer. The two nursery slopes in Chamonix town – Le Savoy (green runs only) and the steeper Les Planards (green, blue and red runs) – are the natural place for young novice skiers (and even sledges) while both Le Tour and Les Houches are very child friendly and have plenty of mellow slopes on which children can learn and progress. Peaceful Les Houches in particular is a good place for families to stay.

The valley has plenty of parks and playgrounds dotted around, as well as activities like mini-golf, bowling, indoor climbing and ice skating, which are always good for older children. See **Other things to do** for details. If you need equipment for kids, you can find children's sunglasses in **Solaris** (p.103), on the main square, and for clothes head to **Snell Sports** (p.103). Skis and snowboards can be rented from **Coquoz Sports** at the western end of the main street or **Sanglard Sports** at the eastern end of town opposite the Place du Mont Blanc. For those who wish to have their own gear you can even buy must-have, dead-cool kids snowboards at specialist snowboard shop **Zero G** (p.103).

Accommodation
Accommodation is undoubtedly the most important factor when planning a ski holiday with children. Who really enjoys carrying all the gear miles to the ski school and lifts? Here are some ideas for child-friendly places to stay, which offer practical advice and services to make your holiday run more smoothly.

maddogski.com

Chamonix

Les Aiglons ***
t +33 (0)4 50 55 90 93
w aiglons.com
270 Avenue Courmayeur.
Sister hotel to Le Morgane, Les Aiglons has also enjoyed recent refurbishment and is now a solid 3-star hotel. The interior is modern, while the new spa ensures relaxation after a long day on the piste. Suitable for families thanks to the outdoor, heated pool and enormous kid-friendly atrium.

The Alpina Hotel***
t +33 (0)4 50 53 41 28
w bestmontblanc.com
Place du Mont Blanc at the eastern end of town.
Conveniently placed between the two nursery slopes; Le Savoy is

---

Checklist for booking family accommodation

- how close are the nearest ski school and lift? Is there a shuttle bus? Do staff escort children to ski school?
- are there price reductions for children?
- are cots, high chairs and baby monitors provided? Can they be hired?
- can rooms accommodate extra beds?
- are rooms for children available away from noisy communal areas?
- are adjoining rooms available?
- are baths available in addition to showers?
- what childcare is available? What vetting is performed and what is the child to adult ratio?

BEST MONT BLANC
CHAMONIX

Plus près des Étoiles

HOTELS RESORTS

FOR BEST RATES...
WWW.BESTMONTBLANC.COM

around five minutes' walk, while Les Planards is a 10 minute walk or one stop on the bus (the bus stop is right outside the hotel).

Argentière
Hotel Grands Montets ***
t +33 (0)4 50 54 06 66
w hotel-grands-montets.com
340 Chemin des Arbérons, Argentière.
A charming, family friendly 3-star in Argentière within two minutes of the ski school Panda Club (see below) and close to the base of the cable car. Further details can be found on page 24.

Les Houches
Les Hauts des Chavants ***
t 020 8780 8810
w inghams.co.uk
Brilliantly situated on the edge of the piste and just above the Prarion lift, Les Hauts de Chavants is a little chalet village just 300m from the lift and ski school. The 3-star apartments/chalets vary in size so book early to ensure that you get the apartment best suited to your requirements. There is an indoor pool which is open to all residents and popular with the kids. Book through **Inghams** in the UK (see right).

Child-friendly tour operators
Inghams
t 020 8780 8810
w inghams.co.uk
Inghams are a well established tour operator happy to spend time tailoring your family holiday. Representatives in resort have a good deal of local knowledge and are able to help you out with ski schools, lift passes and arranging childcare for your stay.

Esprit
t 01252 618300
w espritski.com
Esprit specialise in family holidays and offer a fully tailored package to suit your family's needs. There are various levels of childcare to choose from and the reservations team will be able to advise you before and after booking your holiday. Children are looked after by professional staff.

Mountain Retreats
t 01635 253946
w mountainretreats.co.uk
A very small, family-run chalet operator offering catered chalets around the valley. With a handful of ankle-biters themselves, Brit ex-pats Veronica and Richard understand the needs of a family abroad and are more than happy to help arrange every aspect of childcare. They can provide high chairs, safety gates etc. as well as renting (for a small charge) kids' ski clothes. These extras go a long way to ensure that the holiday is fun-filled and stress-free.

Childcare

Baby Cham
t +33 (0)6 14 55 52 87
w baby-cham.com
The valley's biggest babysitting agency, with something of a monopoly in the market. They're dedicated to providing a flexible service which allows parents child-free time while on holiday. Expect to pay around €20 an hour. Call Ellie, who will be happy to discuss your requirements and find you a suitable nanny.

Ski School

Evolution 2
t +33 (0)4 50 55 90 22
w evolution2-chamonix.com
Regarded as the best independent ski school in the valley, Evo 2 offer fabulous dedicated services for children. Most courses are run from the Panda Base Camp in Argentière, where the children are well looked after and groups decided based on age and ability. Courses and lessons for children aged three to 17 years.

Activities

For details of good non-skiing activities for kids, see **Other things to do** (p.97).

Restaurants

For places that are particularly good for children see **Food and drink** (p.67). Our child-friendly choices show this symbol:

The list – sounds boring but it has all the important information that you don't need until you need it...

Banks and bureau de change

Since Chamonix is more of a town than a resort, the high street is packed with banks, currency-exchange places and cashpoints. As you'd expect in France, banks are closed on Sundays. The most central cashpoint is at the Post Office in Place Balmat and there's a currency exchange just opposite.

Buses

The bus system in Chamonix is extensive, with all of the villages served by some kind of bus. Skis and snowboards are carried on the inside. Bus stops have timetables and route information on them but make sure you check the date as off-season buses are much less regular, and sometimes bus stops are not updated. Buses are free with a Carte d'Hôte card (free from your hotel or chalet). Night buses are thin on the ground, with only two buses after 8pm. Night owls need to organise a taxi (expensive), or walk (cold).

Car hire

The only car hire is **Europcar** (opposite the station, +33 (0)4 50 53 63 40). Cars are in demand and often sold out so prices tend to be higher than those at Geneva airport.

Car parking

There's an €11 fine for parking in a town bay without a ticket (payable at the Police Municipale). It's better to try the free parking at Les Planards, an enormous outdoor car park. Whatever you do, don't park on a zebra crossing – it's tantamount to murder in France!

If you park badly enough, your car will be towed and will end up at one of the towing agencies' impounds. Arve Dépannage is towards Les Praz.

Arve Dépannage
t +33 (0)4 50 55 90 91

Childcare

Babycham
t +33 (0)6 14 55 52 87
w baby-cham.com
Flexible childcare arrangements, full time or part-time, including evenings. The company provides nannies from around €20 an hour.

Mad Dog Ski Chamonix

Churches

Chamonix has two main churches; a Protestant chapel opposite the train station in the middle of town, and a large Catholic church across the square from the tourist office.

Dentist

Alison Pernollet
t +33 (0)4 50 55 54 00
10 Avenue Mont Blanc, Chamonix (on the crossroads just up from the Super U supermarket).
Recommended English dentist.

Doctor

See **Health** below.

Electricity

France operates on 220v; most UK appliances should work with an adaptor (the two round pin type).

Emergency numbers

These numbers can be called from landlines or payphones. If you're on a mobile, you'll need to use the international number 112 as your emergency line.

Medical SAMU – 15
Police (Gendarmes) – 17
Fire (Pompiers) – 18

Mountain Rescue (PGHM)
t +33 (0)4 50 53 16 89
Radio 154,4625 Mhz
The Peloton de Gendarmerie de Haute Montagne are the guys who turn up in the helicopter when you get into trouble up the mountain. They are the heroes of the valley, who you hope you'll never meet (except maybe in a bar).

Events

There's always something going on throughout the season, from the Winter Ride off-piste races organised by **Evolution 2** (p.49) to free glacier awareness and crevasse rescue courses sponsored by mountaineering firm **Petzl**. Various kids' contests are held in Les Houches, often focused around the jumps and rails of the Air Park Bellevue.

The Nissan Outdoor Games film competition is held in Chamonix every year. Less official, but still of note in its own right, is the moonlit Vallée Blanche descent every full moon over the winter. This is one for which you'll certainly want to take a guide (p.43). Lower down, the Chamonix ice rink hosts regular ice hockey

The list

maddogski.com

games which are only a few euro to enter and a lot of fun.

A regular event is the market; a tangy taste of local life served up every Saturday morning from 9am-1pm. You'll find it in the Place du Mont Blanc, next to the fire station. Traders have fruit and vegetables, dried meats, antiques and bric-a-brac to offload; great for gifts and souvenirs.

Towards the end of the season there are plenty of things happening as seasonnaires and visitors alike try to make the most of the last snow. The Freeride Day at Les Grands Montets in April has parapente and wingsuit demos, ziplines, a slalom and of course a rail contest.

Garages

Garage Edelweiss
t +33 (0)4 50 54 53 27
*1069 Avenue Alpages,
Les Houches.*
A Renault dealer with a large workshop and good reputation.

Garage Gorduche
t +33 (0)4 50 54 03 52
*2100 Route d'Argentière,
Argentière (on the left as you're leaving town in the direction of Chamonix).*
Officially a Ford garage but they will work on other makes of car for reasonable prices.

Health

If you need to go to hospital after an accident on the mountain you'll be taken down by helicopter or sled to Chamonix hospital. The costs will be covered by a Carte Neige or your insurance. Once at hospital, your European Health Insurance Card (**nhs.uk**) will cover most expenses and your insurance should top up the rest. Normally people pay for treatment and claim it back once they get home.

For less serious cases, the medical centre in Chamonix is excellent and the standard of care extremely high. There is an x-ray department just next door.

X301 BLACK SCORPION | £40.00

VM11 WHITE VENOM | £30.00

BLOC

For further information contact:

Bloc Systems Ltd
The Base, Daux Road,
Billingshurst,
West Sussex RH14 9SJ
T: 01403 787826
E: info@inline-uk.co.uk

www.bloceyewear.com

Chamonix Hospital
t +33 (0)4 50 53 84 00
509 Route des Pélerins, Chamonix.

Doctors

Dr Yann Hurry
t +33 (0)4 50 54 08 55
125 Rue Charlet Straton, Argentière (towards the bottom of the main hill, opposite the train station).

Dr Alain Richard
t +33 (0)4 50 55 80 55
275 Rue Allobroges, Chamonix (down the hill from the train station).

Dr Roncin
t +33 (0)4 50 55 85 74
Cabinet Medicale, 10 Avenue du Mont Blanc, Chamonix (left out of the Super-U, on the corner at the crossroads).

Internet

The tourist office has free daytime wifi. **McDonald's** and **Chambre Neuf** (p.85) are also popular free-access hotspots for your smartphone. If you haven't got one of those, your best bet is **Mojo's** (p.79) opposite the Post Office.

Laundry

Self-service laundrettes ('laveries') can be found in Chamonix (one in the Alpina shopping centre on Place du Mont Blanc; another behind the Petit Kitchen restaurant in Place Poilu, near the war memorial), Les Houches (Avenue des Alpages) and Argentière.

Mad Dog Ski Chamonix

Lost property

If something goes missing stop by the Police Municipale (see under **Police** below), who seem to accumulate most of the forgotten jackets, wallets etc.

Pharmacy

For non-urgent health problems, stop by a pharmacy. There are plenty all over the valley, easily identifiable by the green cross outside. French pharmacies are like mini-GPs, and will gladly discuss injury or illness. A good central one is:

Pharmacie des Alpes
t +33 (0)4 50 53 15 45
53 Rue du Docteur Paccard, on the main street between the Post Office and Snell Sports.

Physiotherapists

Most physios in Chamonix speak English. They offer a range of services including massage, taping, rehabilitation and laser therapy. Expect to pay €35 for a 20 minute massage or €75 an hour for a physio at your chalet or hotel.

Magic Hands
t +33 (0)6 32 30 38 57
w magichandsphysio.com
Mike and Debbie are an English couple, both physios, who offer competitive prices on massage services in your hotel or chalet.

Physi
t +33 (0)6 82 51 14 01
w physi-chamonix.com
Experienced physios will travel to your accommodation.

Physioinnovation
t +33 (0)6 78 53 68 02
w physioinnovation.com
124 Rue Joseph Vallot.
Bjorn is a Danish physio who speaks great English and has a practice in the centre of town.

Police

You'll come across a couple of different types of police:

Police Municipale
t +33 (0)4 50 53 75 02
Emergency after hours number
+33 (0)6 25 42 02 32
48 Rue de l'Hôtel de Ville (behind the town hall, down the street next to Ogier Sports), 8.30am-12pm, 2-5.30pm.

maddogski.com

The local town police force are responsible for writing parking tickets, telling off noisemakers and dealing with lost property.

Gendarmes
t +33 (0)4 50 53 00 55
111 Route de Mollard, 20m uphill from the roundabout at the base of the Mollard hill, behind the tourist office on the way to the Planpraz gondola.

The state Gendarmes are most similar to the British police, looking after more high-level incidents. If you have something stolen you'll need a report from them for your insurance company.

Post Office
Place Balmat, in the centre of town, 9am-12.30pm, 1.30-6pm. There are smaller branches in Les Bossons, Les Praz and Les Houches.

Radio
Surprisingly, Chamonix does not have an English-language radio station. Most cars and hire shops seem constantly tuned to the babble and chart music of Radio Mont Blanc (97.4FM).

Safety/Theft
In general Chamonix is safe. Like any town there are thieves about, the most frequent losses being skis or boards from outside restaurants. Take particular care around the mid-station restaurants at Le Tour, Brévent and Les Grands Montets. Your best protection is to use a lock. There have also been reports of equipment being lifted from balconies (notably in Chamonix Sud) and jackets being taken from bars.

Smoking
You can buy cigarettes from tabacs. Smoking is not permitted inside public places in France, but most bars have heated outdoor terraces with tables and ashtrays.

Taxis

Getting around by taxi is an expensive business. The rank is beside Chamonix train station, but the drivers leave once the trains have finished, meaning you'll have to call to book one. Expect to pay at least €20 for a transfer in Chamonix town and around €35 to Argentière.

Alp Taxi
t +33 (0)6 81 78 79 51

Taxi Buton Michel
t +33 (0)6 07 19 70 36

Telephones

To call the UK from Chamonix, dial 0044, then drop the first zero and dial the number as normal.

Train

You'll find Chamonix train station in the town centre, sandwiched between the **Chambre Neuf** bar and the Montenvers rack-and-pinion railway sightseeing trip.

The SNCF train line, the Mont-Blanc Express, winds its way from Le Fayet through Servoz, Les Houches, Taconnaz, Les Bossons and Les Pelerins to Chamonix. From there, it calls at Les Praz, Les Tines, La Joux, Argentière, Montroc and Vallorcine. The train terminates at Le Châtelard on the Swiss border. After that, the line goes to Martigny then opens up the rest of the Swiss rail network.

The train is a convenient and reliable way of getting around – for free with your Carte d'Hôte pass – and less crowded than the bus.

Toilets

There are toilets at every cable car station and mountain restaurant. In town, public toilets are located in Place de Mont Blanc, behind the fire station.

Tourist office

The tourist office in Chamonix is hugely efficient and multi-lingual. You'll find them in Place de l'Eglise (**chamonix.com**).

Water

It's fine to drink the tap water in Chamonix, though inexpensive bottled water is widely available.

Weather

See p.47.

maddogski.com

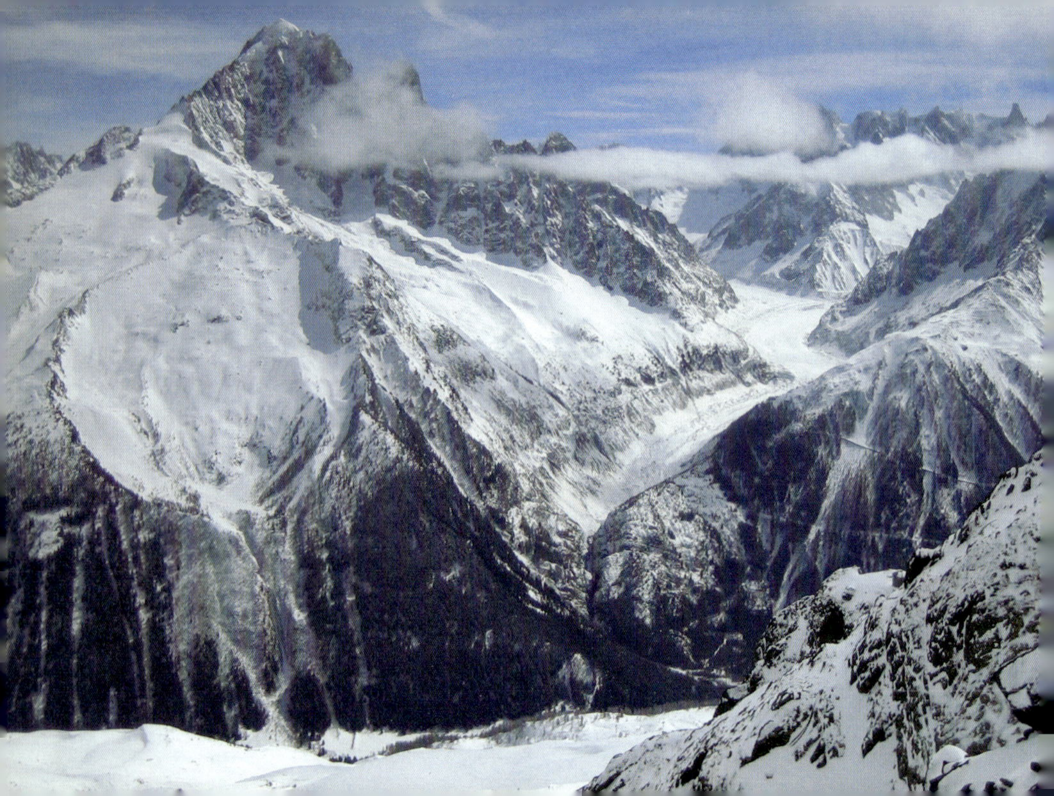

Index

A

Accommodation 21
Activities 97
Aiguille des Grands Montets 92
Airlines 16
Airport 14
   transfer to/from 16
Annapurna 74
Après-ski 82
Argentière 19
L'Arrete Bougnete 92
Art gallery 100
Atmosphere restaurant 74
Avalanches 38

B

Babysitters 112
Bakeries 70
Banks 114
Bar'd Up 83
Bars 82
Beginner slopes 35
Belouga 74
Bergerie 89
Le Bistro des Sports 75
Boarders 44
Board hire 51
Bowling 97
Brévent
   about 29, 40
   mountain restaurants 89
Budget restaurants 67
Bureau de change 114
Buses 114

C

La Cabane 82
Cafeteria Plan Joran 93
Cafeteriere du Lognan 93
Car hire 114
Casa Valerio 75
Casino 97

Emergency numbers

These numbers can be called from landlines or payphones.
If you're on a mobile, you'll need to use the international number 112 as your emergency line.

Medical SAMU – 15	**Mountain Rescue** (PGHM)
Police (Gendarmes) – 17	**t** +33 (0)4 50 53 16 89
Fire (Pompiers) – 18	**Radio** 154,4625 Mhz

Cashpoints 114
Le Caveau 77
Chalet de Charamillon 92
Chalets 25
Chalette 94
Chambre Neuf 85
Childcare 112
Children 107
Churches 115
Cigarettes 120
Cinema 97
Climbing 98
Courant d'air 94
Crèmerie du Glacier 93
Cross-country skiing 45
Cuisine 68

D

Le Dahu 81
Day trips 58
Dentist 115
Doctor 118
Dog sledding 98

E

Restaurant Eden 82
Elevation 1904 77
Emergency numbers 115
Equipment hire 49

F

Families 107
La Flégère
 about 30, 40
 mountain restaurants 89
La Flégère Cafeteria 92
Food and drink 66

G

Le Garage nightclub 85
Garages 116
Les Grands Montets
 about 32, 37
 mountain restaurants 92
Gym 99

H

Health 116
Helicopter rides 99
Heli-skiing 43
Hospital 116
Hotel le Prarion 94
Hotels 21
Les Houches
 about 20, 33
 mountain restaurants 94

Mad Dog Ski Chamonix

Index

I
Ice skating 99
L'impossible 77
L'Imprevu 78
Insurance 116
Internet access 118

K
Kids 107

L
Le Lapin Agile 85
Laundry 118
Lift passes 46
Lost property 119

M
Mad Dog - contact us 7
Maps
  après-ski 84
  mountain restaurants 90
  restaurants 72
  valley 18
  village 22
Mer de Glace 101
Micro Brasserie de Chamonix 86
Midnight Express 78
Mix 86
Mojo's 79
Monkey bar 86
Mountain guides 43
Mountain restaurants 89
Munchie 79
Munster 87
Museum 100

N
Nannies 112
Newspapers 104
Nightlife 82
Night skiing 30
Non-skiing activities 97
Nursery slopes 35

O
Off-piste 37

P
Le Panoramique 92
Paragliding 100
Parking 114
Pharmacy 119
Physiotherapist 119
Piste map 35
Piste ranking 51
Pizza Hop 80
Pizza Salsa 80
Poco Loco 80
Police 119
Post Office 120
Le Pub 87

maddogski.com

R

Refuge Lognan 93
Restaurants
  Resort
    Chamonix 74
    Argentière 81
    Les Praz 81
  Mountain
    Brévent-Flégère 89
    Les Grands Montets 92
    Les Houches 94
    Le Tour 92
Les Rhodos 89
The Rusticana 81

S

Safety 39
Satsuki 80
Shopping
  clothes 103
  food 102
Sightseeing 101

Ski
  area 29
  hire 49
  night 30
  off-piste 37
  school 48
Slalom Bar 88
Snow shoe hiking 101
South Bar 87
Supermarkets 102
Swimming 99
Symbols, guide to 73

T

Take-aways 67
Taxis 121
Telephones 121
La Terrace 87
Toilets 121
Le Tour
  about 20, 32, 41
  mountain restaurants 92
Tourist office 121
Tour operators 21
Trains 34, 121
Transfers 16

U

Using this book 8

V

Vallée Blanche 42
Vegetarians 67
Les Vieilles Luges 94
Villages 19

W

Weather 47
Website 8